A CONCISE GUIDE TO TEACHING WITH
DESIRABLE DIFFICULTIES

THE CONCISE GUIDE TO TEACHING AND LEARNING SERIES

Series Editors: Diane Cummings Persellin and Mary Blythe Daniels

A Concise Guide to Improving Student Learning: Six Evidence-Based Principles and How to Apply Them

By Diane Cummings Persellin and Mary Blythe Daniels

Foreword by Michael Reder

A Concise Guide to Teaching With Desirable Difficulties

By Diane Cummings Persellin and Mary Blythe Daniels

Foreword by Mary-Ann Winkelmes

A CONCISE GUIDE TO TEACHING WITH DESIRABLE DIFFICULTIES

*Diane Cummings Persellin
and Mary Blythe Daniels*

Foreword by Mary-Ann Winkelmes

STERLING, VIRGINIA

Published by Stylus Publishing, LLC.
22883 Quicksilver Drive
Sterling, Virginia 20166-2019

Library of Congress Cataloging-in-Publication Data
Names: Persellin, Diane, author. | Daniels, Mary Blythe, author.
Title: A concise guide to teaching with desirable difficulties /
Diane Cummings Persellin and Mary Blythe Daniels; foreword by
Mary-Ann Winkelmes.
Description: First edition. | Sterling, Virginia : Stylus Publishing,
LLC., 2018. | Series: Concise Guide to College Teaching and
Learning | Includes bibliographical references.
Identifiers: LCCN 2018018382 (print) | LCCN 2018035477
(ebook) | ISBN 9781620365021 (Library networkable
e-edition) | ISBN 9781620365038 (Consumer e-edition) |
ISBN 9781620365014 (paperback : acid free paper) | ISBN
9781620365007 (cloth : acid free paper)
Subjects: LCSH: Learning, Psychology of. | Motivation in
education. | Effective teaching. | Success--Psychological aspects.
Classification: LCC LB1060 (ebook) | LCC LB1060 .P449 2018
(print) | DDC 370.15/23--dc23
LC record available at https://lccn.loc.gov/2018018382

13-digit ISBN: 978-1-62036-500-7 (cloth)
13-digit ISBN: 978-1-62036-501-4 (paperback)
13-digit ISBN: 978-1-62036-502-1 (library networkable
e-edition)
13-digit ISBN: 978-1-62036-503-8 (consumer e-edition)

Printed in the United States of America

All first editions printed on acid-free paper
that meets the American National Standards Institute
Z39-48 Standard.

Bulk Purchases
Quantity discounts are available for use in workshops and
for staff development.
Call 1-800-232-0223

First Edition, 2018

To my husband, Bob, for your quick wit,
delicious meals, and steadfast support throughout
the writing of this book and always.
DCP

To my lively muses, Yakob and Cathey,
and
to the faculty and staff at Glendover Elementary School for
their commitment to and compassion for all children.
MBD

CONTENTS

FOREWORD

Like the first book in this series, *A Concise Guide to Improving Student Learning: Six Evidence-Based Principles and How to Apply Them*, this welcome new contribution provides teachers an invaluable service by summarizing recent research about learning and teaching and then going further to offer practical strategies for applying the new knowledge to teaching practice. In this book, the focus is on (a) understanding new findings about desirable difficulty in learning and (b) identifying a concise set of best practices for teaching with desirable difficulty in responsible, evidence-based ways that will benefit students' learning.

The stakes are formidable. Desirable difficulties can offer inclusive, confidence-building learning opportunities that benefit all students and even help to close achievement gaps. But not all difficulty is desirable or helpful to students' learning. A lack of shared understanding about the purposes, tasks, and criteria for their academic work, for example, can cause the kind of cognitive stress that is not desirably difficult, the kind that diminishes equitable opportunity by excluding some students, threatening their confidence and sense of belonging, and reducing their capacity to learn. The responsibility weighs heavily upon faculty to understand and apply desirable difficulty in helpful and productive ways as they work to advance students' success equitably.

This book concisely offers precisely what's needed to help teachers understand and apply desirable difficulty successfully. The needs of underserved and at-risk students, an important and rapidly growing new majority population of college students, are the focus of chapter 5 in which the authors identify the importance of desirable difficulty for closing achievement gaps and then enumerate teaching strategies designed to encourage these students to embrace the benefits of difficult learning experiences. In other chapters, the authors address student resistance to difficulty and recommend teaching practices that help students to recognize some difficulties as desirable opportunities to practice and acquire lifelong success strategies. The recognition of such learning opportunities that often arrive in the form of challenges is at the center of a growth mind-set.

Each chapter includes a summary of foundational research findings about desirable difficulty in learning and teaching, and a brief, practical set of evidence-based instructional applications as well as an annotated bibliography for readers who wish to look further into the evidence. In addition, two workshops rethink the earlier versions that appeared in *A Concise Guide to Improving Student Learning* in light of recent research on desirable difficulty and its benefits for learning. An appendix, essentially a third workshop, considers beneficial applications of desirable difficulty in online teaching contexts.

As teachers, we aim to facilitate students' learning by guiding their work and increasing their metacognition as they practice skills and acquire knowledge. We want our students to achieve the goals we set for them in our own courses, and we want them to become effective learners with lifelong learning skills that fuel their successes long after they complete our courses. It is gratifying for us and for our students when the teaching/learning process feels easy. Yet ease does not always guarantee deep or lasting learning. Some difficulty can inspire both teachers and students to adopt habits of persistence and innovative, flexible, problem-solving approaches which in turn lead to richer and longer-lasting learning. Understanding and applying desirable difficulty to our teaching in a beneficial, evidence-based way is critical to the equity and success of our students' learning experiences in our courses and beyond. This book equips us with the essential understanding, evidence, and recommended actions we need for adjusting our teaching practices to bring the benefits of desirably difficult learning experiences to our students in a responsible and equitable way.

Mary-Ann Winkelmes
Director, Instructional Development and Research,
University of Nevada, Las Vegas;
Senior Fellow, Association of American Colleges & Universities; and
Director, Transparency in Learning and Teaching
in Higher Education (*TILT* Higher Ed)

PREFACE

This concise guidebook on desirable difficulties is designed to be a resource for academics who are interested in engaging students according to the findings of peer-reviewed literature and best practices but who do not have the time to immerse themselves in the scholarship of teaching and learning. Our book, intentionally brief, is intended to (a) summarize recent research on five aspects of desirable difficulties, (b) provide applications to the college classroom based on this research, (c) include special sections about teaching strategies that are based on best practices, and (d) offer annotated bibliographies and important citations for faculty who want to pursue additional study. We hope that our book will provide a foundation that will assist instructors to teach, using evidence-based strategies that will strengthen learning and retention in their classrooms.

ACKNOWLEDGMENTS

We would like to give special thanks to Beatrice Caraway, Sarah Lashley, Robert Persellin, and Lesley Wigglesworth for reading and commenting on chapters of this book. Helen Emmitt, a special thanks to you for your timely and insightful comments on our introduction. We would like to thank Kaelyn Wiles for letting us use her excellent example of community-based learning in her research methods class. We also want to thank Ellen Prusinski for pointing us toward community based learning resources. This book would have never been completed without a steady stream of folks who stepped up and helped with the care of Yakob and Cathey during these last months. Rick Axtell, Julie Beale, Tim Culhan, Janice James, and Steve and Linda Froehlich, thank you for hours of entertaining Yakob and Cathey, for the homework completed, haircuts given—all the things that made these last months happen. And, of course, thanks to the stellar sitters Annalise Bernardino, Becca Kelly, and Lexy Kos. A special appreciation to the Women Writers Accountability Group for their weekly inspiration and constant support. Finally, we would like to thank our institutions, Trinity University and Centre College, for their support of our work.

INTRODUCTION

Why Make Learning Difficult? An Overview

We often seek to eliminate difficulties in learning to our own detriment.
—Jeff Bye (2011)

"Desirable difficulties" are disadvantages that force an individual to adapt and be better prepared against future difficulties.
—Malcolm Gladwell (2013)

This concise guidebook aims to be a resource for instructors who are not content to have their students memorize material, but instead want them to grapple with challenging problems. Indeed, the very words *grapple* and *challenging* suggest that difficulties are part of how we deal with complex material. In the last 20 years, much peer-reviewed research has emerged about the use of desirable difficulties or making learning intentionally more challenging for better long-term retention. This scholarship has the potential to affect our teaching dramatically. However, few have the time or inclination to delve into this literature. Adjuncts, teaching assistants, instructors, and professors are all necessarily occupied with the demands of teaching, research, and service. For this reason, we have made available a resource that synthesizes peer-reviewed literature and explains teaching strategies in an easy-to-read format.

We intend our guidebook to summarize recent research on desirable difficulties and to present a holistic approach to making our classes more challenging, given the realities of a semester. Each chapter presents an overview of a different aspect of desirable difficulties, followed by various possible applications for the classroom. These teaching strategies are rooted not only in theory but also in practice. We have tried to include applications from a diverse range of disciplines, including sciences, social sciences humanities, arts, and preprofessional programs. Teachers can implement most of these strategies without extensive preparation. We encourage instructors to adapt them according to specific needs, interests, and classroom contexts. The chapters conclude with a short annotated bibliography of the research, which informs these practices for those who want to do further reading. Our hope is that this book will be a resource that will aid instructors in making informed choices about their teaching, based on research and theory.

Desirable Difficulties

Instructors hope to have challenging and engaging classes in which students will not simply regurgitate the information they have received but, instead, transfer their new knowledge and skills to other contexts and situations. Often, as educators, we ask ourselves, "How can we engage students in complex challenges? How can we better help students see connections? How can we help students learn to organize and integrate new information and to think critically and creatively about their own thought processes?"

There are, of course, no easy answers to these questions. They seem to be asked over and over, from generation to generation. Indeed, theorizing about education goes back to Socrates and even before his time. Just as Socrates was responding to the teaching of the sophists, so each new theory must respond to what has gone before in a way that is appropriate for the students of that era. Given the challenges of our time, our purpose in this book is to draw on current research about learning to help answer some of these important questions. Our project expands on the work of investigator R.A. Bjork's (1994) research on "desirable difficulties" and the subsequent work of other investigators in this field (e.g., Diemond-Yauman, Oppenheimer, & Vaughan, 2011; McDaniel & Butler, 2011; McNamara, Kintsch, Songer, & Kintsch, 1996; Roediger & Karpicke, 2006).

In his seminal work, R.A. Bjork (1994) describes desirable difficulties as the practice of creating a situation or condition that initially makes learning more difficult to encode but in the long term easier to retrieve and apply. He advocates posing challenges to the learner that at first slows down the learning process in order to enhance long-term performance. In other words, he wants to add hurdles to the early phases of learning to produce better long-term results. As cognitive psychologist Jeff Bye (2011) notes, these difficulties invite "a deeper processing of material than people would normally engage in without explicit instruction to do so" (para. 3). R.A. Bjork and subsequent investigators advocate that learning be made more challenging in the following ways:

- Retrieval practice: Although students learn from studying for an exam, R. A. Bjork (1994) notes that the act of retrieval itself promotes long-term retention and performance. For example, in a study by Karpicke and Blunt (2011), students had to construct maps based on scientific material learned in class. One group of students was allowed to do so using their notes, the other was not. On a follow-up exam, the group that worked from memory far outperformed the other group.
- Space practice or review sessions: Repeated exposure to material over time increases retention. Current studies indicate that the longer the gaps between study sessions, the stronger the retention (Carpenter, Cepeda, Rohrer, Kang, & Pashler, 2012; Dedrick & Stershic, 2015).
- Interleaving study: Alternating several concepts or skills over a short period of time increases long-term performance (Rohrer & Taylor, 2007).
- Varying conditions of practice: Learning material in multiple ways allows the brain to encode a memory more deeply (Smith, Glenberg, & Bjork, 1978).
- Providing intermittent rather than continuous feedback: Although students need to receive feedback on their work, surprisingly some studies are now showing that a *slight* delay in feedback produces better long-term retention (Hattie & Timperley, 2007).

Although initially implementing desirable difficulties may be frustrating for both students and instructors, ultimately they will benefit the learner. For example, the research of Rohrer, Dedric, and Stershic (2015) revealed that increased challenges during a math class produced better long-term performance. They conducted a 3-month study teaching students slope and graph problems either through interleaving (teaching different skills in the same session) or blocking (teaching skills sequentially). In order to determine understanding and retention of material, 2 follow-up exams were conducted, 1 day later and then 1 month later. On the test given 1 day later, scores for participants trained using interleaving were 25% higher; 1 month later they were 76% percent higher.

When exposed to desirable difficulties, it is not uncommon for the learner to initially make more errors or forget an important process. However, as cognitive scientist Jeff Bye (2011) notes, it is this forgetting that actually benefits the learner in the long term; relearning forgotten material takes demonstratively less time with each iteration. The subjective difficulty of processing disfluent information can actually lead learners to engage in deeper processing strategies, which then results in higher recalls of those items.

By forcing the brain to create many retrieval paths, a desirable difficulty makes the information more accessible. If learners can use information in multiple ways and multiple contexts, they are able to build many paths to memory; thus, if one path is blocked, they can use another.

However, implementing desirable difficulties into our practice can be challenging. Learners, of course, are gratified when they feel they are processing information easily. Instructors understandably want learning to come quickly for students and may be tempted to choose a method that produces immediate results. We propose that teachers and students need to focus less on immediate success and more on deeper understanding. Bye (2011) has stated that when instructors facilitate learning by making the process easier, it may increase short-term performance and feelings of success, but it may also decrease long-term retention. In fact, making learning too straightforward can mislead students into thinking they know more than they do. Current research indicates that allowing students to feel confusion and frustration early in the learning process encourages stronger long-term retention and performance (Bjork, 2017; E. Bjork & R. Bjork, 2011; Diemand-Yauman, Oppenheimer, & Vaughan, 2011; Karpicke & Blunt, 2011). Indeed, the iterative process required in our struggle to learn is a key in helping novice learners become independent, creative, and sophisticated thinkers. Finally, asking students to struggle in our classes also helps make students tolerant of things they might not understand right away, finally making learning more interesting.

The Zone of Proximal Development

The danger in demanding much from our students is not knowing when it is too much. The task must be something students can accomplish or the difficulty becomes undesirable. Students who become frustrated or disengaged may want to give up on our classes, even, perhaps, our discipline. Is there a "sweet spot" in learning where students are simultaneously challenged and gratified? Soviet psychologist and social constructivist Lev Vygotsky (1978) believed so when he developed his theory called the Zone of Proximal Development (ZPD). Vygotsky stated that the level of difficulty that is desirable is just past what the person has already mastered. That "sweet spot" is just beyond the student's grasp—not so easy that it results in boredom and not so hard that the learner quits (Fani & Ghaemi, 2011). When students grapple with challenges just beyond mastery, it is what Kapur (2014; see also Kapur & Bielaczyc, 2012) refers to as a productive struggle because learners can eventually see the rewards of their efforts. When students grasp the concept that struggle often leads to accomplishment, it sets up a pattern of success in which learning becomes intrinsically rewarding and pleasurable. As instructors place what students may perceive as roadblocks in their paths, it is important to remember the balance between challenge and reward. Metcalfe (2009) noted that this balance can result in labor with gain rather than labor in vain.

Desirably Difficult

Shifting the educational norm from pellucid delivery, which makes learning seem easy, to situations in which students must learn to navigate ambiguity can incite student resistance. For this reason, we have also tried to contextualize desirable difficulties with the realities of teaching. We understand the importance of teaching evaluations for contract renewal, tenure, and promotion. We have tried to offer a work that not only synthesizes the robust research in the area of desirable difficulties but also provides practical ways to implement them in our practice. For this reason, half of this book is devoted to elaborating the well-researched aspects of desirable difficulties: retrieval practice, spacing and interleaving, and perceived setbacks. The other half, also evidence-based, presents instructors with ways to help students have an optimal mind-set for facing challenges, ideas for incorporating desirable difficulties with at-risk students, and ideas to navigate student resistance. For those who are interested in incorporating desirable difficulties into their online courses, our appendix includes a workshop dedicated to those specific challenges.

Chapter 1 sets the stage by citing the research of Carol Dweck (2006) on growth mind-set. Our hope is that if we foster a growth mind-set in our students—that is, they understand that abilities are malleable and can be improved with effort—then they will be more likely to take the risk to navigate challenges posed in our classrooms. Included in this chapter is a discussion of the importance of acquiring grit and perseverance as students work through challenging tasks (Duckworth, 2016).

Chapters 2 and 3 address the nuts and bolts of retrieval practice, spacing, and interleaving. In chapter 2, we synthesize research on memory and recall and its relationship with struggle. The more effort it takes to retrieve information, the better the information is stored. We examine the efficacy of the testing effect: Karpicke and Blunt (2011) cite testing, self-testing, and practice testing as being more beneficial to learning than all other nontesting review practices (e.g., study, review, rereading, feedback and concept maps). Chapter 3 explores spacing, repeated exposure to material over time (the opposite of cramming), and its corollary, interleaving, which refers to studying different topics or subjects in a short time. In fact, Cepeda, Coburn, Rohrer, Wixted, Mozer, and Pashler (2009) conducted 2 studies showing that spacing study improved recall up to 150% during a 6-month period. We also discuss strategies for incorporating spacing and interleaving into course design.

When students encounter difficulties in their work, they will often stumble and become discouraged. Our tendency as instructors may be to feel compelled to rescue or help students instead of requiring them to solve the problem themselves. Chapter 4 delves into working with students as they encounter setbacks. We discuss ways to help students learn from failure and how to reward them for doing so. Chapter 4 also elucidates Kapur's (2012) notion of productive failure and grapples with the question of when delayed feedback is appropriate. The chapter concludes with a workshop based on best practices for instructors who wish to implement problem-based learning into their courses.

Chapter 5 addresses using desirable difficulties when teaching first-year and at-risk college students. There is strong research that demonstrates that desirable difficulties and high-impact practices help close the achievement gap. We offer strategies to increase the structure and support of course material for these students. Such practices include having students interact with faculty and peers about a substantive matter over a relatively long period of time and low-stakes testing. We also provide resources for instructors who wish to implement community-based learning in their courses.

Our final chapter addresses to what degree difficulty is desirable and how and when to utilize it. We present research about student resistance and provide strategies to navigate pushback from students. This chapter discusses the importance of student feedback and offers suggestions to avoid pitfalls when implementing a new teaching technique.

Readers of our first book will note that we have updated and incorporated our workshops on problem-based learning and community-based learning in this book. We did so because we believe these two topics are crucial to a discussion of desirable difficulties and because readers need to be able to access these workshops without having to refer to our previous book. We hope that the bibliographies, annotated studies, instructional applications, and written workshops we provide will guide the interested reader to a fuller understanding of desirable difficulties. Finally, we, of course, realize that not every strategy in the book is suitable for everyone. There is no one teaching strategy that will ensure student success. Our goal is to provide a foundation that will assist instructors in making informed decisions about their teaching and course design.

I

TEACHING A GROWTH MIND-SET

It's not that I'm so smart, it's just that I stay with problems longer.
—Albert Einstein

*Talent is overrated; effort (or practice, or
self-discipline) is what really counts.*
—Geoff Colvin

Chapter 1 shares current research on growth mind-set and grit as well as strategies for helping students develop resilience in order to persevere when confronted with deliberately difficult challenges.

Growth Mind-Set

Why are some students determined to persevere when working on difficult content while others become discouraged? Why are some learners convinced that they are not cut out to succeed in some subjects, such as math or art? What can instructors do to encourage students to become more resilient and to learn from their mistakes? How can instructors support students as they work through frustration? One way is to help students develop what Carol Dweck (2006) refers to as a "growth mind-set." This book begins with a discussion about growth mind-set because it plays a key role in helping students navigate challenges and setbacks. A growth mind-set allows students to persevere in classes where instructors are asking them to struggle with deliberately difficult problems.

Carol Dweck (2006), the psychologist who pioneered the concept of growth mind-set, identified two ways of thinking about our intelligence and ability to succeed. The fixed mind-set is a belief that our abilities are innate. When people believe that they have fixed or native abilities, they may not see the point in trying harder. Why exert effort if you can't see a marked improvement? For example, someone with a fixed mind-set may believe she simply can't sing and is therefore unlikely to join a choir, not wishing to be embarrassed among more talented musicians and preferring to invest her time in an activity that feels more comfortable. The fixed mind-set demands that people strive to look smart to their peers—to seem as though their skills come naturally rather than through hard work and practice. The fixed mind-set may lead learners to avoid challenges in order to conceal their deficiencies.

In contrast, a growth mind-set refers to a belief that abilities are malleable and can, with effort, be improved. People who hold a growth mind-set about intelligence, for example, may feel that they can become smarter by studying and challenging themselves to learn material they find difficult. A growth mind-set, says Dweck (2006), creates a passion for learning unhindered by fear of making mistakes; mistakes are simply another learning opportunity. People with a growth mind-set tend to embrace challenges and difficulties. They believe that hard work and learning from setbacks are the keys to their success. As Ken Robinson (2006), speaker and educator, said, "If you're not prepared to be wrong, you'll never come up with anything original" (p. 27).

While acknowledging that we possess a mixture of both fixed and growth mind-sets, Dweck (2006) encourages us to strengthen our growth mind-set. She also reminds us that a growth mind-set results from more than just hard work. Students also need effective instruction from educators. For example, a failing student who tries harder by doing the same thing over and over may feel even more inept if not shown new and better strategies.

It is important to distinguish the growth mind-set from the self-esteem movement in the 1990s. This movement attempted to make students feel good about themselves and their prospects for academic success through positive feedback (Dweck, Walton, & Cohen, 2014). Unfortunately, telling students that they were smart or talented did not significantly motivate them (Heckman, Stixrud, & Arzua, 2006). Mueller and Dweck (1998) found that praising students' innate talent rather than encouraging their efforts backfired. Complimenting students for their intelligence taught them that ability was fixed, which created vulnerability. However, providing feedback on students' efforts and the strategies they used both promoted a growth mind-set and fostered resilience.

Molden and Dweck (2006) have found four factors that affect students' persistence and growth mind-sets:

1. Their beliefs about themselves as capable learners
2. Their skills as self-regulators or their ability to control and change their own behavior
3. Their academic and personal goals
4. Their perceptions of their social connectedness to others

Capable Learners

In fact, simply teaching students about a growth mind-set can improve their performance. In a five-year study, Blackwell, Dweck, and Trzesniewski (2007) found that students who learned about the malleability of intelligence had higher academic motivation, better behavior in school, and significantly better grades in mathematics. Although both boys and girls benefitted from the intervention, it turns out that teaching a growth mind-set went a long way to close the longstanding gender achievement gap in mathematics. Girls who received the growth mind-set intervention slightly exceeded boys in math scores, whereas girls in the control group who did not receive the intervention performed well below the boys. In their study, instruction time for this intervention totaled just three hours and was a powerful tool for improving students' academic motivation and achievement. Paunesku and colleagues (2015) also found that carrying out a growth mind-set intervention significantly raised semester grade point averages in core academic classes (see the Annotated Research section at the end of this chapter).

Self-Regulation

Dweck (2006) advises instructors to encourage effort. Ask them, "What did you learn from your hard work on this project?" or, "You worked hard on this problem, but it didn't work. What's the big take-away?" By reflecting on their growth as learners, students may develop more grit and persistence. They realize that by changing their behavior they can change the outcome. Moreover, this process entails developing problem-solving skills. Students need to assess what has not been working and brainstorm alternative strategies. Effective problem-solvers brainstorm to find solutions and figure out a way to turn things around.

Students have also shown greater motivation to learn when they believe their learning ties into their professional goals and when their work has meaning and value. For example, Hulleman and Harackiewicz (2009) found that students were more interested in their science courses and made better grades when they were asked to make connections between their lives and what they were learning. When a task is important and related to some aspect of our lives, we tend to have more stick-to-itiveness. Because meaningless projects have less personal buy-in, students should be encouraged to determine strategies to make a topic relevant to their experience or interest.

Stephens, Hamedani, and Destin (2014) and Walton and Cohen (2007) point out that students are more motivated when they feel psychologically safe and connected to others. Feeling safe allows them space to explore and become more capable learners. Cultivating motivation, of course, is key when we are working with desirable difficulties. Students who are motivated and feel connected may be more willing to engage with difficult tasks and to take emotional risks.

Grit and Growth Mind-Set

An idea related to growth mind-set is referred to as *grit* by author Angela Duckworth (2016). She defines *grit* as a combination of passion and perseverance for a singularly important goal. She claims that what matters the most is sticking with things and working consistently to improve. In her research, she has found that grit is not only a good indicator of success but also a trait that can be developed. While the research is still relatively new, Duckworth claims that we all have the power to increase our inner passion, perseverance, and resilience to become more successful. Duckworth (2016) cautions, however, that "it's not resilience if you're just trying the same thing over and over and expecting change. Trying hard isn't enough; being resilient means you're also willing to try differently" (p. 193).

Regarding Duckworth's interviews of people she believed to be "paragons of grit," she says many of them had a formative experience that inspired them, whether it was rowing on their college crew team or a grueling semester with a tough teacher. "When you can say, 'At least this isn't as hard as that'—that's true grit" (Duckworth, 2016, p. 108).

Instructional Applications

Break It Down

Students are more likely to persevere when an important long-term goal is broken down into smaller achievable goals or bite-size pieces so that the task does not seem to be overwhelming. Dividing a large research paper into sections and then determining a workable timeline to tackle each section works well for many students. Preparing for a senior music recital by scheduling shorter, more informal concerts with friends can be a good way to scaffold this major goal. Accomplishing smaller goals will increase one's rate of success, lead to accomplishing bigger goals, and ultimately increase confidence in learning.

Stress the Idea That Ability Is Malleable and Can Be Developed

Share Dweck's (2006) work with students to illustrate that skills and knowledge are not fixed, but can be strengthened.

Make It Worthwhile for Students to Learn From Their Mistakes

Give a cumulative final examination and allow students to replace a lower grade with their final exam grade if they demonstrate that they have mastered the concept. Such practices encourage students to see setbacks as opportunities to rethink the problem and to try again. Remind students to try to learn from their mistakes rather than ignoring useful negative feedback.

Encourage Effort and Active Reflection

Ask students to reflect on how they learned from their mistakes as well as their successes. Urge them to see that effort is the path to mastery. When students succeed, focus on the effort, the learning strategies, and the value of learning rather than solely on the success. If students have failed, ask them to reflect on what went right and what went wrong; then, have them come up with a plan. What strategies can they try that would improve their performance? If they try these, make sure to reward their effort. When their effort leads to mastery, point this out to the student.

Create a Culture of Respect

Students are more likely to persist when instructors respect them and have high expectations for success. When academic support is needed, instructors are encouraged to offer it in ways that feel supportive rather than punitive.

Try Problem-Based Learning

In a problem-based learning model, students develop competencies through engagement in long-term, challenging, or real-world problems that require planning and monitoring. Projects can be aligned with students' interests and passions (Barseghian, 2013). Students may be more motivated and successful when working in small cooperative learning groups rather than competitive groups. A sense of responsibility to the group can encourage a growth mind-set (see Workshop 4.1, Problem-Based Learning).

Use Stories to Inspire

Share case studies about students who have struggled. Invite students to offer advice to others who are facing challenges based on developing knowledge of the growth mind-set. Conversely, find lessons from the success of others rather than feeling threatened by the success of others.

Share Stories of Your Own Failure With Students

Smith College's program, Failing Well (Bennett, 2017), sponsors a campaign to destigmatize failure and awards certificates to students when they fail. Similarly, over a dozen colleges and universities have formed a Resilience Consortium (2017) on the Internet that features stories of failure, setbacks, and struggles. It also shares resources and programs to encourage students when they need reassurance. Other models include the Success-Failure Project (Bureau of Study Counsel, n.d.) at Harvard, the Princeton Perspective Project (n.d.), and Penn Faces (n.d.) at the University of Pennsylvania.

Challenge Students to Think With A Growth Mind-Set

In Dweck's (2014) first-year seminar course, she challenges students to do something with an "outrageously growth mind-set." She reports that one painfully shy student ran for dorm president and won.

Encourage Students to Find Strategies to Make a Topic Relevant to Their Experience or Area of Interest

When a task is important and related to some aspect of our lives, we will tend to have more stick-to-itiveness. Instructors can also share stories or refer students to literature that can help make topics more relevant to them (see Workshop 5.1, Community-Based Learning).

Remind Students That Grit Can Be Acquired

Duckworth stresses that grit can be developed, like a muscle (Engber, 2016). The more students exercise their grit and tenacity, the easier it can be to call up that work ethic when needed. The feeling of "I can't do this" is more quickly replaced by, "I can do this, and this is how I will do it." After a frustrating assignment, ask students to do a one-minute writing session to reflect on their effort. Afterward, divide students into small groups to discuss their "what is next?" strategies for mastery.

Cultivate the Trait of Conscientiousness in Your Students

Ask students to keep a writing journal or a lab log to monitor how conscientious they are in working toward their goals. Remind them to focus on resilience and growth rather than perfection.

Encourage Learners to Engage in Positive Self-Talk

When students state that they cannot do a task, have them rephrase the statement to explain a possible first step.

Show Students Duckworth's (2013) Six-Minute TED Talk and Discuss in Class

Have students take Duckworth's (2013) 10-question grit scale. Ask students if they agree that this is an accurate assessment of their grittiness. Based on the TED Talk and the scale, ask students their ideas for increasing their grittiness.

Annotated Research

Aronson, J., Fried, C., & Good, C. (2001). Reducing the effects of stereotype threat on African American college students by shaping theories of intelligence. *Journal of Experimental Social Psychology, 38*(2), 113–125. doi:10.1006/jesp.2001.1491

Seventy-nine college students were assigned either to a control or growth mind-set group. The growth mind-set group viewed video clips of how the brain, and hence intelligence, is capable of growing. These same students then participated in writing and discussion exercises, focusing on the malleability of intelligence. Results showed that students in the growth mind-set group reported significantly higher grade point averages than their peers in the control group. Nine weeks after the intervention had concluded, the growth mind-set group also reported significantly higher academic engagement and greater enjoyment of the course material. When students considered intelligence to be changeable and malleable rather than a stable and fixed entity, it resulted in greater academic achievement.

In a 5-year study, Blackwell, Dweck, and Trzesniewski (2007) replicated and applied Aronson and colleagues' (2001) experiment with 373 students in 4 successive seventh-grade classes in New York City. These students also learned about the malleability and growth potential of intelligence by reading and discussing a science-based article that described how intelligence develops. A group of seventh-grade students served as the control group and learned memory and mnemonic strategies unrelated to growth mind-set. The students who learned about intelligence's malleability and growth potential had higher academic motivation, better academic behavior, and significantly better grades in mathematics than the control group. Additionally, girls who received the growth mind-set intervention slightly exceeded the boys in the control group in math grades, whereas girls in the control group performed well below the boys. The findings are important because instruction time for the intervention totaled just 3 hours. This study suggests that this can be a cost-effective method for improving students' academic motivation and achievement.

Duckworth, A. L., Quinn, P., & Seligman, M. (2009). Positive predictors of teacher effectiveness. *Journal of Positive Psychology, 4*(6), 540–547.

This study examines why some teachers are more effective than others and concludes that traditional indicators (such as certification) do not account for teaching success. In this longitudinal study, investigators asked 390 novice teachers, placed in underresourced public schools, to complete a report on their explanatory style (i.e., was it optimistic?), their grit, and their overall well-being prior to the school year. At the end of the school year, teacher effectiveness was measured in terms of student academic gains. Results indicated that those teachers with positive traits were better able to perform. It further suggests that positive traits could be considered in the selection of teachers.

Paunesku, D., Walton, G. M., Romero, C. L., Smith, E. N., Yeager, D. S., & Dweck, C. S. (2015). Mindset interventions are a scalable treatment for academic underachievement. *Psychological Science, 26*(6), 784–93.

Although many of the research studies focus on younger learners, this is a large-scale study of 1,594 students in 13 geographically diverse high schools. Students were assigned to a control group or a growth mind-set group. Students in the growth mind-set group were presented with an article that focuses on the fact that setbacks in school provide opportunities to learn rather than indicate limited potential. Students were then asked to summarize what they learned from this article and instructed to apply this knowledge to a case study of a hypothetical student who thought he was not smart enough for school. Among the students who accounted for the bottom third of students in the sample, the growth mind-set interventions significantly raised the semester grade point average in core academic classes. Interestingly, although many of the studies conducted about growth mind-set have focused on the science, technology, engineering, and mathematics (STEM) areas, this one focused on the core course areas: English, social studies, mathematics, and sciences.

Robertson-Craft, C., & Duckworth, A. L. (2014). True grit: Trait-level perseverance and passion for long-term goals predicts effectiveness and retention among novice teachers, *Teachers College Record, 116*(3). Retrieved from http://www.tcrecord.org/Content.asp?ContentId=17352

In two longitudinal samples, novice teachers assigned to schools in low-income districts followed a seven-point rubric to rate their grit. The rubric assessed perseverance and passion for long-term goals based on information regarding college and work experience from new teachers' résumés, SAT scores, college grade point average, and interview ratings of leadership potential at the time they were hired. Grittier teachers outperformed their colleagues in teaching assessments in the classroom. Grittier teachers were also less likely to leave their classrooms mid-year.

2

RETRIEVAL PRACTICE AND TESTING

A Key to Learning and Retention

Repeated retrieval of learned information not only strengthens information in our minds but builds the foundation for adapting to the world around us.

—Eric Rees (2016)

Chapter 2 shares recent research and strategies about how instructors can help students boost retrieval for long-term retention. We discuss how we store and recall memories and the importance of prior knowledge for recall and the testing-effect.

When retrieval practice is challenging, it can create meaningful learning that is long lasting and coherent and promotes problem solving (Karpicke, 2016). As educators, we devote much of our attention to helping students attain new information, concepts, and ideas; however, recent research in neuroscience suggests that we also boost knowledge by requiring the learner to retrieve information. Karpicke (2016) explains that retrieval practice is essential for long-term retention, problem-solving, and integrating complex concepts. It is imperative, of course, to differentiate this from rote learning or simple memorization, which is "short-lived, poorly organized and does not support the ability to transfer knowledge" (Karpicke, 2016, para. 12).

Memory and Retrieval

How well we store information will affect how well we recall it. For example, what we ate for lunch yesterday may be easy to recall today, but next week it may not be. Since we did not need the information, we did not store it well in the first place. As Terada, Sakurai, Nakahara, and Fujisawa (2017) state, not all memories are created equally because "the more connections neurons have to other neurons, the stronger the memory" (Terada et al., 2017, p. 249). The authors give a clear example of what they mean by asking the reader to remember two sets of letters: (a) NPFXOSK and (b) ORANGES. They explain that readers of English will remember the second set of letters. We have not only a linguistic context for the word *oranges* but also a sensory memory of them. By activating relevant experiences, we can help students better store and therefore better retrieve information (Zull, 2002).

Retrieval strength measures how likely we are to recall something immediately and how close the memory is to the surface of the mind. Storage strength measures how deeply that memory is rooted (Bjork, 2011; E. Bjork & R. Bjork, 2011). When recalling a memory, the event is retrieved from long-term memory, moved to working memory, and then stored back in long-term memory. (Although *recall* and *retrieval* can be used interchangeably, retrieval targets the effort to find information in order to recall it.) Each time we retrieve a memory, we have the potential to create stronger associations with relevant experiences, prior knowledge, or linguistic contexts. The more we access information, the easier it is to recall (this is why it is easier for many of us to remember our PIN number, while it seems virtually impossible to remember the algebra we learned in high school). Because storage strength is so capacious (it is limitless), it makes the ability to retrieve a memory all the more important.

Retrieval and Effort

Information that is learned quickly and without the benefit of review and retrieval practice may boost short-term performance, but long-term retention will suffer. Why? Because when the information is easily accessed, we actually sacrifice storage strength. This is why, for example, cramming has high short-term retrieval strength, but low storage strength. When learners have to make an effort to retrieve information, it reinforces the memory (Brown, Roediger, & McDaniel, 2014). What this means for our students is that repeating and rehearsing newly acquired information are often counterproductive. When we employ rote learning we may facilitate short-term retrieval, but we and colleagues (Brown et al., 2014) point out, in order to keep retrieval routes strong, learners need to establish "powerful *retrieval cues* that can reactivate the memories" (p. 100) through repeated use of the information.

So how do we boost retrieval and storage strength in learning? This is where desirable difficulties can come into play. Instead of repetitive drills focused on newly learned material, it is better for learners to space their practice. The time that elapses between sessions allows the learners to forget. When we relearn the information, it actually makes the learning stronger. Forgetting and then relearning creates the potential for stronger storage in long-term memory or, in other words, deeper learning (E.L. Bjork & R.A. Bjork, 2011). As Peter Brown and colleagues (2014) note, "One of the most striking research findings is the power of active retrieval—testing—to strengthen memory, and that the more effortful the retrieval, the stronger the benefit" (p. 17).

Asking strong and thoughtful questions in class is an excellent retrieval strategy to assess retention, understanding, and application. Nilson (2016) suggests opening a discussion with a few *remembering* stage questions (who, what, where, and when) as a mental warm-up. Instructors can then follow these questions by moving to the *understanding* stage, which checks for comprehension and allows time to clarify misconceptions. Students should then be ready to respond to *application* questions, which require problem-solving. Finally, they can *evaluate*, or critique, the strengths and shortcomings of the argument and then *create* their own model.

Retrieval and the Generation Effect

The generation effect is directly related to retrieval. It refers to the finding that people who have taken an active part in producing information recall that information better than those who have it provided for them. When learners are asked to generate target material through an active, creative process, rather than simply by passively reviewing, their retention increases. These active strategies include generating words or phrases, completing sentences, and creating questions in the margins when reading. This effect has been recognized in memory research for over 40 years (Jacoby & Chestnut, 1978; Slamecka & Graf, 1978). Since that time, the generation effect has proven to be robust in the recall of word lists (McDaniel, Waddill, & Einstein, 1988) and in reading comprehension (DeWinstanley & Bjork, 2004; Wittrock & Alesandrini, 1990).

Importance of Retrieval for Learning: The Testing Effect

Of course, students have to learn information in order to retrieve it. However, once students have been introduced to new information, their time is better spent trying to retrieve the material instead of rereading it. For example, the meta-analysis of Adesope, Trevisan, and Sundararajan (2017), which examined practice testing, found that "practice tests are more beneficial for learning than restudying and all other comparison conditions" (p. 659). Karpicke and Blunt (2011) found that when students were asked to construct concept maps based on scientific material they had studied, the group that constructed the maps from sheer recall outperformed those who used their books when they created their maps. Butler (2010) found that repeated testing produced superior trans-fer of learning than did repeated studying. These findings are all consistent with the testing effect, a phenomenon in which repeated, spaced retrieval (or self-testing) of newly learned material promotes long-term retention of information, a way that is far superior to using repeated study sessions (Seekers et al., 2016).

It turns out what is most effective is what good teachers and learners already do: homework problems and examples, self-tests, and frequent short quizzes. Being asked to retrieve information or testing strengthens memory, learning, and retention. New information can then become recallable in the future. While many educators assume testing is a way to assess informa-tion, it is also a powerful learning tool in and of itself. Testing requires the brain to retrieve information from long-term memory, which makes future retrieval quicker (Bjork, 2011). Moreover, testing and recall shows you what you know and do not know. This allows students to know where to focus their study. Additionally, recalling what you have learned causes your brain to reconsolidate the memory (it strengthens its connections to prior knowledge) and "makes it easier for you to recall the memory in the future" (Brown et al., 2014 p. 202). The tried-and-true "testing effect" is a powerful one.

What types of quizzes or retrieval tests work the best? Strong exam ques-tions and in-class questions increase retrieval strength and result in deeper learning (Anderson & Krathwohl, 2001; Black, Harrison, Lee, Marshall, & William, 2003, 2004). Instructors are encouraged to ask both lower level and higher level questions when planning instruction and assessment. Lower level questions deal with recalling and remembering facts, while higher level ques-tions involve evaluating and creating (Bloom & Krathwohl, 1956). Bloom and Krathwohl (1956) designed a tiered model of classifying thinking and questioning, which was later revised by Anderson and Krathwohl (2001). The categories of Bloom's revised taxonomy (Anderson & Krathwohl, 2001), with examples of key verbs, are as follows:

> *Remembering (lowest level)*: Recalling, defining, listing, describing
> *Understanding*: Interpreting, inferring, paraphrasing, classifying,
>   summarizing
> *Applying*: Implementing, using, executing

Analyzing: Comparing, organizing, deconstructing, attributing, outlining
Evaluating: Checking, critiquing, judging, testing
Creating (highest level): Designing, constructing, planning, producing

Bjork (2011) found even the use of multiple-choice tests to be effective. Why? When students are not sure of the correct answer, it forces them to retrieve information. Even if the students retrieve information that pertains to the wrong answer, it is a useful exercise. Just recalling prior knowledge to determine the best answer of those offered can lead to increased retrieval strength and subsequent long-term retention.

If testing, practice testing, and self-testing are key to long-term learning, why don't more students use these techniques when they study? Karpicke (2016) speculates that students confuse meaningful retrieval practice with rote learning. He suspects that students use recall as a knowledge-check "to see if they know something, rather than out of the belief that practicing retrieval itself boost learning. Unfortunately, many students use a 'once-and-done' strategy" (Karpicke, 2016, para. 11). Perhaps if instructors demonstrate the benefits of the testing effect, learners will be more likely to take advantage of this tool.

Instructional Applications

The following strategies are suggested to instructors to incorporate additional active retrieval practices into their teaching.

Multiple Repetitions and Rehearsals of New Information

Multiple repetitions can strengthen learning when students are forced to recall the information rather than reread it. It is also important that students vary the manner in which they rehearse the information. When students are asked to recall and rehearse information in a variety of contexts, they demonstrate greater retrieval strength. A way to incorporate different contexts in the classroom could include creating a structured debate based on the new information where students must take a stand and defend their assigned viewpoint. Have students turn to a peer to explain and/or give an example of what was just learned in class (Baume & Baume, 2008).

Find Meaningful Patterns to Organize the Framework for Learning

Learners tend to recall patterns and overall meaning before they remember specific details (Medina, 2014). Ask students to step back to consider the big picture. Invite students to transfer the pattern learned to a case study shared in a previous class. Have them use analogies.

Give Students Time to Process Information

Learners require time to store new information in long-term memory. Giving students a brain break in class can often be beneficial following an intense period of learning new information. After a 20-minute lecture on new material, break into small groups to discuss what was presented or to work on a group problem or case study involving the new material. Have students participate in a think-pair-share activity to change the dynamics in the class.

Reactivate Fading Memories When Introducing a New Topic

Ask students to make connections to the new material. This strategy will help students access neural networks to activate prior knowledge to make the topic more relevant (Zull, 2002). This strategy also allows instructors to assess the level of prior knowledge and to correct misconceptions.

Make Learning Relevant

Facilitate learning by connecting new learning challenges to students' interests, prior knowledge, and skill levels. Educators are encouraged to show students the relevance of their studies to professional, disciplinary, and "real-world" concepts via guest speakers and field trips (Kember, Ho, & Hong, 2008). Community-based learning can also be an excellent tool (see Workshop 5.1).

When students are more engaged in the learning process, they see the relevance of their studies to professional, disciplinary, and/or personal contexts (Berkley, 2010; Prince, 2004; Willingham, 2009).

Use Stories, Analogies, and Metaphors

These real-world examples make learning engaging, relevant, and memorable for learners. Students report that the stories are often the most easily recalled part of a presentation.

Ask Students to Free Write

In the first few weeks of the term, give students writing assignments in which they are asked to organize what they know about the material in the class. This gives the instructor the opportunity to address misconceptions.

Use Pretests

Pretests introduce a new topic or unit in order to strengthen long-term learning. Although pretest performance is predictably poor because students have not yet been introduced to relevant information, they nonetheless strengthen subsequent learning. The process of pretesting can provide cues for the learner about what information will be key (Kornell, Hays, & Bjork, 2009).

Encourage Students to Use Self-Tests

Self-tests provide valuable feedback about what students have learned and what they have forgotten. Initially, the instructor can create quizzes. Gradually encourage students to create their own tests to help them recall what important materials were discussed in class.

Give Entrance Quizzes at the Beginning of Classes

These quizzes can be helpful to both the instructor and the student as a quick review of the reading assignment or what was discussed in previous classes. Brief written quizzes, verbal quizzes with hands or thumbs raised, or quizzes administered with clickers all work well. In addition, they serve as low-stakes assessments and are helpful early in the learning process before the student receives a major grade.

Give Mid-Class Quizzes

These serve as lecture breaks and provide time to review material before introducing a new topic. They also force students to recall pertinent information.

Give Exit Quizzes

These review quizzes also serve as effective closure to a class. They let both the instructor and students know what was learned in class and what needs more review.

Have the Learner Use Flashcards to Self-Test

The two-step process of creating and then using the flashcards requires the learner to reflect on the salient points of the topic. The self-testing with flashcards gives the learner immediate feedback. Free flashcards can be created online using such programs as Cram and Quizlet.

After Introducing a New Concept, Ask Students to Transfer This Idea to a New Situation

In order to promote long-term recall, regularly ask students to apply, evaluate, and/or transfer newly presented material. Deeper learning is fostered when students put additional effort into organizing and retrieving information.

Space Learning Sessions Rather Than Mass Them

This will help increase retrieval strength (Baddeley & Longman, 1978; Dempster, 1990). (See chapter 3 on spacing and interleaving.)

Have Students Generate or List Major Ideas

This active approach boosts recall more than simple review, and it can be used both to open a class discussion or serve as a review of the discussion (McDaniel & Butler, 2011).

Combine Text With Images

Vision is a strong aid for organizing and remembering materials. For example, in a meta-analysis, Ginns (2005) reviewed 43 experimental studies and found that students who studied material that combined text and graphics performed significantly better than students who studied from text alone. Bui and McDaniel (2015) found that giving students a skeletal outline or a diagram before a lecture strengthened free recall and short-answer performance (Medina, 2014; Pieters & Wedel, 2005; Stenberg, 2006).

Peer-to-Peer Explanations

As we know, learning by doing is an effective means to learn material. Have students explain difficult concepts to one another.

Annotated Research Studies

Adesope, O., Trevisan, D. A., & Sundararajan, N. (2017). Rethinking the use of tests: A meta-analysis of practice testing. *Review of Educational Research, 87*(3), 659–701. doi:10.3102/0034654316689306

This meta-analysis compares practice testing to "non-testing learning conditions." The investigators conclude that practice testing is highly effective and, in fact, "more beneficial for learning than restudying and all other comparison conditions" (Adesope, Trevisan, & Sundararajan, 2017, p. 659). This article's conclusion deals with the practical and theoretical implications of practice testing that are especially useful for educators.

Atkinson, R. C., & Shiffrin, R. M. (1968). Human memory: A proposed system and its control processes. In K. W. Spence & J. T. Spence (Eds.), *The psychology of learning and motivation* (Vol. 2) (pp. 89–195). New York, NY: Academic Press.

Atkinson and Shiffrin proposed their widely respected model of how memory works. They stated that memory consists of three separate and distinct storage systems:

1. Sensory memory
2. Working or short-term memory
3. Long-term memory

According to the model, new information is received by our senses (sensory memory); if the learner is paying attention, it is quickly converted into a type of code that is stored in working memory.

Bertsch, S., Pesta, B., Wiscott, B., & McDaniel, M. (2007). The generation effect: A meta-analytic review. *Memory & Cognition, 35*(2), 201–210.

The investigators conducted a meta-analysis of studies on the generation effect, which included 86 studies with 445 measures and a total of 17,711 participants. The generation effect resulted in better memory for both older adults and younger adults. The generation effect is especially robust for recall of numbers and words.

Dunlosky, J., Rawson, K., Marsh, E., Nathan, M., & Willingham, D. (2013). Improving students' learning with effective learning techniques: Promising directions from cognitive and educational psychology. *Psychological Science in the Public Interest, 14*(1), 4–58.

The authors offer descriptions and recommendations of about 10 learning techniques. Their findings indicate that practice testing and distributive practice are beneficial to learners of different ages and across disciplines. They have been shown to boost student performance in a variety of contexts.

Karpicke, J., & Blunt, J. (2011). Retrieval practice produces more learning than elaborative studying with concept mapping. *Science, 331*(6018), 772–775. doi:10.1126/science.1199327

This study found that taking a practice test before an exam better prepared students than other methods of studying—including rereading the passage. Two hundred college students were divided into four groups and asked to read several paragraphs about a scientific topic. Each group performed one of the following learning strategies:

1. Reading the text for five minutes
2. Reading the text in four consecutive five-minute sessions
3. Drawing diagrams about information from the excerpt they were reading
4. Reading the passage once and taking a retrieval practice test, requiring them to write down what they recalled

A week later, all four groups took a quiz asking them to recall facts from the passage they had read and draw conclusions based on those facts.

The students in the fourth group who took the practice test recalled 50% more of the material than in the other 3 groups. The investigators concluded that by organizing and creating meaningful connections and struggling to remember information to identify areas of weakness, students could better recall information.

Kornell, K., Hays, M. J., & Bjork, R. A. (2009). Unsuccessful retrieval attempts enhance subsequent learning. *Journal of Experimental Psychology: Learning, Memory, and Cognition, 35*(4), 989–998. Retrieved from https://bjorklab.psych.ucla .edu/wp-content/uploads/sites/13/2016/07/Kornell_Hays_Bjork_2009_JEP-LMC.pdf

In a series of experiments, the investigators gave college students pretests that "ensured that retrieval attempts would be unsuccessful" (Kornell, Hays, & Bjork, 2009, p. 989). In the test conditions, students attempted to answer the question before being shown the answer; in the read-only conditions, the question and answer were presented together. When posttested, the investigators found that students' unsuccessful retrieval attempts enhanced future learning. The investigators suggested that taking challenging pretests might be one key to effective learning.

Richards, B., & Frankland, P. W. (2017). The persistence and transience of memory. *Neuron, 94*(6), 1071–1084.

This study examines the importance of forgetting as an evolutionary tool. The authors suggest that the interaction between memory and forgetting allows for "intelligent decision-making in dynamic, noisy environments" (Richards & Frankland, 2017, p. 1071). The study provides valuable insight for evidence-based practices to make learning relevant and to cue memory.

Roediger, H., & Karpicke, J. D. (2006). Test-enhanced learning: Taking memory tests improves long-term retention. *Psychological Science, 17*(3), 249–255.

Roediger and Karpicke found that students remembered 61% of information from repeated testing compared to 40% from repeated study. In 2 experiments, students studied prose passages and (a) took 1 or 3 immediate free-recall tests, without feedback, or (b) restudied the material the same number of times as the students who received tests. Students then took a final retention test 5 minutes, 2 days, or 1 week later. When a final test was given after 5 minutes, repeated studying improved recall relative to repeated testing. However, on the tests that were delayed by 2 days or 1 week, prior testing produced substantially greater retention than studying, even though repeated studying increased students' confidence in their ability to remember the material. The investigators stated, "Repeated testing is a powerful means of improving learning, not just assessing it" (Roediger & Karpicke, 2006, p. 249).

Seekers, M. J., Bonasia, K., St-Laurent, M., Pishdadian, S., Winocur, G., Grady, C., & Moscovitch, M. (2016). Recovering and preventing loss of detailed memory: Differential rates of forgetting for detail types in episodic memory. *Learning and Memory, 23*(2), 72–82. doi:10.1101/lm.039057.115

The investigators in this study examined (a) the loss over detailed and central memory over time, (b) the role of cuing for retrieving memories, and (c) the role that retrieval plays in remembering and forgetting. Their findings are interesting for educators because they showed that forgetting is not always permanent and that "retrieving a memory shortly after it was encoded prevented loss of both central and peripheral details, thereby promoting retention over time" (Seekers et al., p. 72).

Van Blerkom, D., Van Blerkom, M., & Bertsch, S. (2006). Study strategies and generative learning: What works? *Journal of College Reading and Learning, 37*(1). Retrieved from https://files.eric.ed.gov/fulltext/EJ747769.pdf

One hundred and nine college students participated in an experiment that involved reading a passage and responding to a 20-item multiple-choice test based on the reading. The students were randomly assigned to 1 of 4 treatments:

1. Reading and copying
2. Reading and highlighting
3. Reading and taking notes
4. Reading and generating questions

Students in the fourth group, who generated questions after reading the material, performed better than the three other groups on the test. The authors attributed this improved performance to generative learning.

Annotated Resources

Terada, Y. (2017, September). Why students forget—and what you can do about it. *Edutopia*. Retrieved from https://www.edutopia.org/article/why-students-forget-and-what-you-can-do-about-it

This is an excellent resource for educators. Terada concisely reviews recent brain-based research on memory and forgetting and then gives examples of teaching strategies based on this research.

3

MIX IT UP TO MAKE LEARNING LAST

The Importance of Spacing and Interleaving

The spacing effect is the finding that information that is presented repeatedly over spaced intervals is learned much better than information that is repeated without intervals (i.e., massed presentation).

—R. A. Bjork (1994)

An effective strategy is to interleave one's study: study a little bit of history, then a little bit of psychology followed by a chapter of statistics and go back again to history. Repeat.

—R. A. Bjork (1994)

I n chapter 3, we share research and applications of two related practices: spacing and its corollary interleaving. In this chapter, we discuss how to implement opportunities for retrieval into courses over a semester by using spacing and interleaving.

Spacing refers to repeated exposure of the same material over time (the opposite of cramming), while interleaving refers to scheduled repetitions of different subjects or different skills during a short period. While varying topics or skills rather than focusing on only one at a time can feel disorganized, the increase in retention can be significant. It may seem counterintuitive to space and interleave instruction, but there is compelling research that supports doing just that.

Spacing Instruction

Studies in cognitive and educational psychology show that repeated encounters with material over time—rather than massed practice (all at once)—produce stronger long-term learning (Bjork & Allen, 1970; Carpenter, Cepeda, Rohrer, Kang, & Pashler, 2012; Cepeda, Pashler, Vul, Wixted, & Rohrer, 2009; Hattie, 2008; Kang, 2016; Roediger & Karpicke, 2011). In fact, Mozer, Pashler, Cepeda, Lindsey, and Vul (2009) found that practice over time has the potential to double retention. These gaps in between study require students to struggle to recall earlier experiences, which will eventually make the information easier to retrieve (Benjamin & Tullis, 2010).

This idea is not new. The spacing effect is one of the oldest and most reliable findings in research on the science of learning. In 1885, German psychologist Hermann Ebbinghaus (1964) was already conducting experiments on the spacing effect, and, in 1899, American philosopher and psychologist William James (1899) was also advocating spaced practice:

> You now see why "cramming" must be so poor a mode of study. Cramming seeks to stamp things in by intense application immediately before the ordeal. But a thing thus learned can form but few associations. On the other hand, the same thing recurring on different days, in different contexts, read, recited on, referred to again and again, related to other things and reviewed, gets well-wrought into the mental structure. This is the reason why you should enforce on your pupils' habits of continuous application. (p. 129)

This advice was offered over 100 years ago and is now bolstered by hundreds of studies with strong scientific evidence. The spacing effect is a robust finding across many area disciplines, and yet, as we will see, most learners believe massed practice is more effective (Bjork, 1994; E. Bjork & R. Bjork, 2011).

Even though instructors have repeatedly warned students not to cram for an exam, we still may be resistant to changing our own course design to allow students to benefit from the spacing effect. As we organize our classes, we often plan in discreet modules, focusing on one topic at a time. To many instructors, spacing topics throughout the term may seem more time-consuming and may feel less organized. However, the long-term benefits can far outweigh the practice of massing information. Recent scholarship (Küpper-Tetzel, Kapler, & Wiseheart, 2014; Rawson & Dunlosky, 2011) has found that when material was studied three more times and the time period between reviews increased, retention was stronger (Carpenter & DeLosh, 2005; Cull, Shaughnessy, & Zechmeister, 1996; Hser & Wickens, 1989;

Landauer & Bjork, 1978; Rohrer, Dedrick, & Stershic, 2015). While the subjects studied and the gaps between reviews varied, all resulted in increased retention. These studies suggest that material should be reviewed within a couple of weeks of the initial lesson, and then again after a month or two.

In order to strengthen learning, E. Bjork and R. Bjork (1992, 2011) recommend that instructors strategically plan to revisit topics throughout the semester. For example, the first review session can occur two weeks after the introduction to the lesson, and the next can be scheduled four weeks later for increased retention. For maximum benefit, they also suggest increasing the length of time between reteaching the topic to the point that it is almost forgotten. Why? Because forgetting can actually benefit the learner. The difficulty the learner feels when trying to retrieve material allows the learner to engage more deeply with the subject matter. And, there is an added benefit. With each iteration, the information becomes easier to retrieve.

Unfortunately, there is no one-size-fits-all approach regarding the timing between learning events for optimal long-term retention. The ideal time between review sessions, of course, depends partly on the strength of the initial learning. However, a good rule of thumb is to remember the goal. If it is to retain information for only a short period of time, spacing gaps of a few days may work well, while if retention is to be achieved over a long period of time, spacing gaps of several weeks to several months may work better (Carpenter et al., 2012). As instructors plan their courses and develop course sequences, they may want to keep in mind that if the goal is preserving important knowledge over a lifetime, spacing gaps of several semesters or years may be best.

How does this look when planning for teaching a course within the realities of an academic semester? In order to encourage students to recall and engage with prior information, instructors should plan to incorporate additional activates a few days or weeks after introducing material. Even assigning homework two to three weeks after a topic has been taught has been found to strengthen learning (Rohrer, Dedrick, & Burgess, 2014). Another way to promote long-term retention is by giving comprehensive exams. However, to optimize the benefit of spacing, instructors should incorporate review activities throughout the semester rather than planning intensive review sessions immediately prior to final exams (Küpper-Tetzel et al., 2014).

To capitalize on the spacing effect, encourage students to distribute their study. Students may be interested to know that researchers (Cepeda, Vul, Rohrer, Wixted, & Pashler, 2008) have referred to cramming as "a perfect prescription for rapid forgetting" (p. 1101). Urge students to schedule multiple practice sessions. In these spaced sessions, students should focus on the quality of understanding rather than the quantity of information that they try to cover. Each time they study, they build on previous learning, which subsequently leads to deeper learning (Bjork, E. L., & Bjork, R. A., 2011).

Combining retrieval practice tests (see chapter 2) with spaced study can also be a potent strategy to enhance learning and memory. Bahrick (1979) dubbed this practice *successive relearning*. Successive relearning involves alternating reviewing with retrieval practice until each item is correctly recalled (Rawson, Dunlosky, & Sciartelli, 2013).

In summary, by spacing instruction and study—whether the study be at fixed or variable intervals—promotes stronger learning and retention. There is solid research demonstrating that spacing teaching and study is more effective than massing (Carpenter & DeLosh, 2005; Carpenter et al., 2012; Dempster, 1988; Francisco, 2015). And, if spacing is combined with retrieval practice (successive relearning), retention can be even stronger.

Interleaving Instruction

Interleaved instruction is mixing or alternating several concepts or skills in the same session or within close proximity. For example, a pianist may alternate between practicing scales, chords, and arpeggios. A Spanish instructor may alternate between teaching the conjugation of a verb, learning new vocabulary words, and reading a poem. The opposite of interleaving is blocking or targeting one concept or skill at a time. For example, the pianist practicing in blocks would only rehearse scales and the Spanish instructor would limit the instruction to conjugating one verb tense.

The first studies addressing the advantages of interleaved practice were found in the domain of motor skills. In 1986, Goode and Magill found that interleaved practice of 3 kinds of badminton serves produced better performance than blocked practice of the same serving skill. Since then, many studies have shown that interleaving is also a successful academic strategy. For example, the research of Rohrer and Taylor (2007) revealed that teaching increasingly difficult versions of the same skill during a math class produced better long-term performance. The authors instructed students how to find the volume of four obscure geometric figures. The first group was taught how to find the volume of a single figure at a time, while the second group was taught how to find the volume of all 4 figures in the same session. Although initially the second group performed worse in practice sessions, after a weeklong delay, they significantly outperformed the first group in a testing session. The group that had received interleaved instruction (i.e., finding the volume of all 4 shapes in the same session) answered 63% of the questions correctly compared to only a 20% correct response rate from the group that received blocked instruction.

Why? Well, we go back to desirable difficulties: conditions that make learning more challenging, especially in the initial stages of learning, which encourages deeper learning. As the Rohrer and Taylor (2007) study shows, in the short-term, asking learners to struggle may slow down performance; however, there is a positive effect on long-term retention.

There are several reasons that interleaving is such a powerful strategy. When instruction is blocked, students often perceive that they understand the material better than they do. In short, students often prefer blocked sessions because they learn more easily and feel they are mastering the material (Kornell & Bjork, 2008). Thus, students may not work as hard on the initial processing, and the material isn't stored as effectively. Interleaving, however the, requires learners to work harder, moving back and forth between concepts (R.A. Bjork, & E.L. Bjork, 2011; Carson & Wiegand, 1979; Yan, E. L. Bjork, & R.A. Bjork, 2016). Moreover, interleaving asks us to use information in multiple ways and multiple contexts, which forces the brain to build many pathways to memory; thus, if one pathway is blocked, we can use another.

However, because interleaving asks learners to struggle, it may lead learners to underestimate their retention. For example, in a study of learning to differentiate artists' styles of painting, Kornell and Bjork (2008) found that 77% of participants were more accurate following interleaved practice than blocked practice. However, a majority of the participants self-reported that they thought that blocked practice was equal to or even better than interleaved practice. What is even more surprising is that participants made these judgments *after* taking the tests that clearly demonstrated the superiority of interleaved practice.

While spacing material is time intensive and may not always be possible over the course of a semester, interleaving several skills or concepts in one session can be more feasible. However, interleaving does require careful planning; it should not lead to chaos, nor should it be interpreted as multitasking (which is not advised). Instructors need to find a balance of how long to spend on a concept or skill before moving to a different one. It is also important for instructors to remember that they do not have to interleave all of their presentations during a class. It is one more tool in the instructors' toolbox. Because learners may initially be uncomfortable when asked to interleave new material or when learning new skills, it is important to share the research on long-term retention with them. Remind students why you are introducing several topics within a single class period rather than focusing on only one. (For specifics about how to negotiate student resistance, see "Teaching Applications" in chapter 6.)

As with spacing, to get the maximum effect of interleaving, encourage students to try this strategy as they study. Initially, encourage students to strive to interleave some of their study and practice before completely changing their study habits. Remind them that while blocked practice may be easier and more efficient in the short-term, it is less efficient for long-term memory or development of skills. Urge students to mix up their practice material because switching between tasks (again as opposed to so-called multitasking) requires students to process information multiple times and in many ways. This practice has the added bonus of helping them not only in your class but also all their classes. Because interleaving has the potential to be frustrating, Jenkins (2013) encourages learners who are interleaving their study to track their progress. Keeping track of the date and times of their study sessions and the results of their quizzes allows students to notice their progress even when they feel like they are struggling.

Instructional Applications on Spacing and Interleaving

Strategically Plan Spacing in the Syllabus

Once spacing, reviews, and retrieval practices are planned and clearly outlined in the syllabus, they are easier to implement. This practice will also help students more easily understand the structure of the course.

Review

Instructors are encouraged to incorporate brief reviews of concepts that were taught in previous weeks. Reviewing material from a previous class can be an effective strategy to open a class session and engage learners.

Something Old and Something New

Include questions in homework assignments that pertain to information discussed several weeks earlier in class. This approach is also useful when class time is limited and regular review is challenging to schedule. This cumulative approach strengthens learning.

Make Exams and Quizzes Cumulative

This approach requires students to continue to review information on their own, which increases retention.

Reboot Class Every 20 Minutes

Organize a class period in 20-minute segments. Focus on teaching a different topic or using a different strategy in each segment. For example, after lecturing on topic A for 20 minutes, invite a discussion on topic B from the previous week for the second 20-minute block, followed by checking homework based on a topic from the previous month. While this will feel awkward at first, the long-term payoff will make it worthwhile.

Weave in Ideas From Previous Discussions

In class discussions, bring up a topic that was addressed a few weeks earlier. Encourage students to discuss it without referring to their notes and to frame it within what they have learned since the previous discussion.

Generate Phrases to Prime the Pump

Ask students to recall phrases and sentences at the beginning of class about a reading or lecture from the previous week's class. List these phrases on the board. Letting students generate phrases is more powerful than having the instructor provide them. Two weeks later, bring up that topic again and challenge the students to recall, once more, the big ideas.

Regularly Ask Recall and Synthesis Questions in Class

Ask students questions on material that was addressed earlier in the semester, but don't let them look at their notes. This makes them struggle to recall information.

Take Time to Demonstrate How to Interleave Several Topics When Studying

Students will need guidance on how to rethink their study patterns rather than cramming.

Encourage Distributed Practice Through Distributed Testing

Instructors can nudge students toward distributed practice through distributed testing. Frequent testing provides strong incentive for regular review.

Use Student-Centered Learning Tools

Encourage students to review by creating their own learning tools such as flashcards, outlines, PowerPoint slides, or MP3s. These tools allow students to repeat, self-test, and review material outside of class that they will need to know for the test.

Annotated Research Studies

Bird, S. (2010). Effects of distributed practice on the acquisition of second language English syntax. *Applied PsychoLinguistics, 31*, 635–650.

In this study, Bird found that longer spacing gaps improved adults' understanding of grammatical rules. Two groups of participants saw 2 similar sentences. One was grammatically correct and the other was not. Their task was to choose the correct version. Practice sessions were separated by 3 days for the first group and by 14 days for the second. When a test was administered 60 days later, the group who practiced the task 14 days after the initial instruction performed significantly better than the group who practiced the task only 3 days following instruction.

Cepeda, N., Coburn, N., Rohrer, D., Wixted, J., Mozer, M., & Pashler, H. (2009). Optimising distributed practice: Theoretical analysis and practical implications. *Experimental Psychology, 56*(4) 236–246. doi:10.1027/1618-3169.56.4.236

In 2 studies that involved 3 laboratory sessions, investigators examined the effects of spacing learning when studying foreign vocabulary words, facts, and names of visual objects. Spacing the study sessions improved final recall by up to 150% within a 6-month period. Both studies demonstrated that test accuracy was sharply increased by increasing the time between study sessions. The investigators also stated that their results confirmed that both cumulative reviews and exams promote long-term retention.

Cepeda, N., Pashler, H., Vul, E., Wixted, J. T., & Rohrer, D. (2009). Distributed practice in verbal recall tasks: A review and quantitative synthesis. *Psychological Bulletin, 132*(3), 354–380.

The investigators examined results of 839 assessments of spaced or distributed practice in 317 studies, measuring students' verbal recall. This study analyzed (a) the effects of massed learning versus spaced and (b) the time period between learning events. The results suggested that as the interval of time between study sessions increased, the retention (as measured by the final test) also increased. More specifically, spaced (versus massed) learning of items consistently showed benefits, regardless of retention interval. Learning benefits increased, however, with increased time lags up to a point. The authors summarize their findings, stating that once the interval between learning sessions reaches a relatively long period of time, further increases either have little effect or may even decrease memory. The retention will vary depending on the strength of the initial learning, the strength of the review sessions, and the length of time before the final test.

Hatala, R., Brooks, L., & Norman, G. (2003). Practice makes perfect: The critical role of mixed practice in the acquisition of ECG interpretation Skills. *Advances in Health Sciences Education 8*(1), 17–26.

Medical students were learning how to diagnose electrocardiogram (ECG) readings. Students were randomly assigned to either the interleaved group where examples from various ECG categories were interspersed or the blocked group where the examples presented were all from a single category and were studied together. The results were that the students who studied the ECG readings using the interleaved approach had superior diagnostic accuracy (46%) compared to 30% accuracy for the students in the blocked session ($p < 0.05$).

Kornell, N. (2009). Optimizing learning using flashcards: Spacing is more effective than cramming. *Applied Cognitive Psychology, 23,* 1297–1317. doi:10.1002/acp.1537

Kornell asked participants to use an Internet-based flash card program to learn GRE-type word pairs. In the first 2 studies, she found that reviewing the full stack of 20 flashcards every day for 5 days (spacing) was more effective than focusing on 4 of the 20 flashcards per day (massing). Spacing was found to be more effective than massing for 90% of the participants. One of the most interesting findings of the study was that 72% of the participants believed that *massed* practice had been more effective than spacing the practice. This study is useful to cite to students because it demonstrates that the learner's perception is not necessarily accurate.

Rohrer, D., Dedrick, R. F., & Stershic, S. (2015). Interleaved practice improves mathematics learning. *Journal of Educational Psychology, 107*(3), 900–908. doi:10.1037/edu0000001

This 3-month study involved teaching seventh graders slope and graph problems. Weekly homework featured either interleaved or blocked designs. Of the 9 participating classes, 5 used interleaving for slope problems but used blocking for graph problems. In order to determine understanding and retention of material, 2 follow-up exams were conducted, 1 day and then 1 month later. On the test conducted 1 day later, scores for participants trained using interleaving were 25% better; 1 month later, they were 76% better. The researchers concluded that interleaving can give learners a significant learning boost to longer retention.

Rohrer, D., & Taylor, K. (2006). The effects of overlearning and distributed practice on the retention of mathematics knowledge. *Applied Cognitive Psychology, 20,* 1209–1224.

College students were assigned to solve an abstract permutation problem. Students were asked to determine the number of permutations of a sequence of items with at least 1 repeated item. For example, the sequence *abbccc* has 60 permutations, including *cabcbc* and *abcbcc*. They were then asked to solve 10 practice problems that were given in a single session (with no spacing gap) or spaced across 2 sessions, 1 week apart (with a 7-day spacing gap). A test with similar problems was given 1 and 4 weeks later. While spacing had no reliable effect on test scores after a 1-week delay, after a 4-week delay, test scores doubled.

Rohrer, D., & Taylor, K. (2007). The shuffling of mathematics problems improves learning. *Instructional Science, 35,* 481–498. doi:10.1007/s11251-007-9015-8

In this study, students were taught how to calculate volumes of 4 obscure geometric solids: wedge, spheroid, spherical cone, and half cone. Students were split into 2 groups, the "interleaved practice group" and the "blocked practice group." The interleavers were given all 4 tutorials and were then asked to complete 16 practice problems that were interleaved (shuffled) so that each set of 4 problems (1–4, 5–9, etc.) included 1 of each type of problem. The blockers were given 1 tutorial and then 4 related practice problems (e.g., wedge tutorial and wedge practice problems) before moving on to the next 3 types, in a similar blocked manner. Both groups completed 2 practice sessions as well as a test, each spaced 1 week apart. The results found that students taught by interleaving the concepts performed 63% better on the final test than students taught by blocking.

4

DON'T HELP THE LEARNER SO MUCH

Teach Students to Learn From Setbacks

If there is no struggle, there is no progress.

—Frederick Douglass (1857)

Chapter 4 outlines the importance of letting students experience set-backs, how and when to curb instructor feedback, and the process of productive failure. The chapter concludes with ways to scaffold learning to better help instructors hit the "sweet spot" between student success and frustration (because a learner who gives up doesn't learn).

Although as educators, we want our students' learning to come easily and smoothly, evidence-based studies suggest that people learn more deeply when they are required to struggle. A large body of research (Hattie, 2012; Kapur, 2012; Kapur & Bielaczyc, 2012) indicates that the struggle to learn increases long-term retention and performance. Indeed, cognitive scientist Jeff Bye (2011) claims that when "instructors facilitate learning by making it easier, it may increase short-term performance, but it may decrease long-term retention" (para. 3). As Terry Doyle (2011) notes, "The one who does the work, does the learning" (p. 7). Although it may, at times, go against the grain of the instructor's desire to help, we allow more learning to take place when we are not helicopter instructors.

This chapter discusses ways in which we can help our students become independent learners. The path may not always be easy—it requires that instructors deliberately allow for frustration in their classrooms, as well as make time and space for iterative learning. This type of teaching necessitates risk-taking on the part of instructor and learner alike.

Deliberately Ambiguous Problems: Creating Situations That Require Critical Thinking and Problem-Solving

One way to ask students to struggle is to create situations that require critical and creative thinking as well as problem-solving. These deliberately ambiguous assignments allow students a chance to think outside the box in a real-world way and in ways in which their regular homework (although important) may not allow. For example, Carrithers, Ling, and Bean's (2008) study of critical thinking in finance majors found that many students were unable to deal with ill-structured problems, even at a very basic level, such as addressing clients' problems or translating financial language to a layperson. Their results suggest that typical homework has not prepared students to confront the messy problems of the real world.

These experiences can take a number of forms, from messy or unstructured problems to high-impact practices. These may include but are not limited to (a) problem-based learning, (b) learning communities, (c) community-based learning, (d) research with a faculty member, and (e) field work. How are they relevant to desirable difficulties? They are all asking students to deal with unpredictable situations, they are time-intensive, and they often require students to tackle problems to which there are no easy solutions. The format for using these practices may vary by discipline and instructor. However, the practices all give students the opportunity to see what they are learning in different contexts and settings and to integrate, synthesize, and transfer knowledge, which is essential for a deep learning experience.

The challenges these high-impact practices present have the potential to increase the students' learning and retention of the material. These ambiguous or messy problems also ask students to "dig, to question, to take risks, to fail (and learn something from that failure that they may not have otherwise learned)—in short, to discover" (Huddler, 2013, para. 3).

What is the role of unstructured and messy problems in the current desire to teach resilience and failure? In order to get to a solution, learners must go through an iterative process; they must learn to both recognize their mistakes and to learn from them, which will serve them long after they have left the academy. One of the products (intentional or not) of messy problems and high-impact practices is that students are put in a position where they may experience setbacks or even need to ultimately (re)solve the problem. Moreover, new studies are now emerging that claim that mind-set and resilience are a major predictor of success (see chapter 1 on the growth mind-set).

The downside of this process? Students are understandably terrified of failure when they are receiving a grade in the course. Rather than thinking of making mistakes or experiencing setbacks as a critical element of learning, they regard them as detrimental. Thus, the job of the instructor is to create a learning culture that values iterative learning and shows students that setbacks are an integral piece of deep and life-long learning.

Fostering Mastery Goal Orientation

As instructors, we know that making errors is key to understanding complexities in our disciplines. However, learners fear mistakes will either hurt their grade or result in embarrassment. One way to help our students understand that setbacks are part of the learning process is to clearly differentiate performance goals and learning goals. Indeed, research in educational psychology has shown that the type of goal a person is working toward impacts how he or she pursues the goal (Ames & Archer, 1988; Dweck & Leggett, 1988). Those with a goal to master learning are willing to make great efforts to achieve that goal, while those with a goal to simply perform a task tend to want to demonstrate tasks they can already do. They may take fewer risks as their goal is to either make a good grade or to look good in the eyes of their peers. Luckily for us, research is pointing out that goal orientation is not necessarily inherent but, instead, may be situational (Wolters, Yu, & Pintrich, 1996). For example, if students believe the instructor values grades, they may be more likely to be performance-oriented, whereas if students see that the instructor values the process, they may be more mastery goal-oriented.

Instructors who want to encourage students to grapple with complex problems and difficult situations should create an environment that fosters mastery goal orientation. One way to do this is to let students know that not all failure is alike. For example, Edmondson (2011) in the *Harvard Business Review* examines the nuances of failure: avoidable failure, unavoidable failure, and intelligent failure. Students should embrace "intelligent failure," or those setbacks that occur when the answer is not yet known but are crucial pieces of the process that ultimately lead to a solution. These types of setbacks force "us to focus on the specific task of determining why the attempt at hand failed" (Burger & Starbird, 2012, p. 48). Rewarding students for learning from their setbacks may help them take more and more risks in the classroom and ultimately help them master the material. (For suggestions on fostering growth mind-set, see chapter 1.)

Productive Failure

Kapur and Bielaczyc (2012) define *productive failure* as a learning design that creates conditions for "learners to persist in generating and exploring representations and solution methods (RSMs) for solving complex, novel problems" (para. 1). In other words, students are given problems and allowed to struggle with them *before* they receive direct instruction about how to solve them. Instructor intervention comes only after students have explored a number of solutions. This carefully designed process is meant to both engage learners and to activate their prior knowledge. It is also a highly collaborative process that creates a safe space for students to compare, contrast, and elaborate on one another's work. The instructor is primarily there as a facilitator. Students are encouraged to present their work to each other with the goal of improving their solutions rather than assessing them.

Kapur and Bielaczyc (2012) have found that this method boosts understanding of complex topics. They focused their study on ninth-grade math students who were learning the concept of variance. One group of students was taught with direct instruction, while the other group was asked to generate solutions before they received direct instruction. On the posttest given to both groups, the second group outperformed the first on conceptual understanding. This study demonstrates that when instructors allow students to explore and generate solutions, they often outperform classmates who received direct instruction early in the learning process. Moreover, although initially their performance is weaker on summative assessments, over the long-term, these students better demonstrate abilities to transfer their understanding from one situation to the next.

This method, of course, is not appropriate for every class and every learning situation. When students have little experience and are novice learners, they do not have sufficient knowledge to generate new solutions. As Brown, Roediger, and McDaniel (2014) point out, desirable difficulties are desirable because they "support learning, comprehension, and remembering. If, however, the learner does not have the background knowledge or skills to respond to them successfully, they become undesirable difficulties" (p. 98).

Scaffolding

As Svinicki (2004) points out, an instructor who understands how the learning process works can help students learn more efficiently. Any time instructors are asking students to struggle, whether it be with ill-structured problems or high-impact practices, we need to be aware of the cognitive skills of the learners. What we might expect from a class of majors will be very different from what we should ask of an intro class. One way to support students while asking them to engage in complex tasks is to scaffold the material. Although struggling leads to deeper learning, frustration to the point of giving up helps no one. There is no "magic bullet" on how to scaffold; this will depend on the discipline and the level of the students. Instructors should remember to give students enough support to move them toward greater and eventually more independent learning. Hmelo-Silver, Duncan, and Chinn (2007) claim that extensive scaffolding is key "to reduc[ing] the cognitive load and allowing students to learn in complex domains" (p. 101). Scaffolding is also crucial if we want students to be able to engage with complex tasks that would otherwise be out of their grasp.

When employing scaffolding, the role of the instructor is to coach or mentor students without explicitly giving them the answers (Hmelo-Silver et al., 2007). As students work through the process, they become increasingly better problem-solvers, and instructors can begin to fade the scaffolding. The instructor's ability to judge the learner's evolving understanding is a key element to the success of this process. As Hmelo-Silver and colleagues (2007) state, "Teachers play a significant role in scaffolding mindful and productive engagement with the task, tools, and peers. They guide students in the learning process, pushing them to think deeply, and model the kinds of questions that students need to be asking themselves, thus forming a cognitive apprenticeship" (p. 101).

Delayed Feedback

Feedback helps students recognize the discrepancy between their actual understanding and their perceived understanding of a topic. The gold standard has been to give students immediate, specific, informative, and behavior-based feedback. However, a growing body of research indicates that in some situations delaying feedback helps long-term retention. To many of us, delaying feedback seems counterintuitive; however, as Brown and colleagues (2014) note:

> in motor learning, trial and error with delayed feedback is a more awkward but effective way of acquiring a skill than trial and correction through immediate feedback; immediate feedback is like the training wheels on a bicycle: the learner quickly comes to depend on the continued presence of the correction. (p. 40)

The authors hypothesize that this may be in part because learners can become dependent on feedback and when they are put in real-world situations, the absence of feedback hinders performance.

Mullet, Butler, Verdin, von Borries, and Marsh's (2014) study published in *The Journal of Applied Research in Memory and Cognition* claims that delayed feedback promotes transfer of knowledge. In this study at the University of Texas, El Paso, undergraduate engineering students received either immediate feedback on completion of an online homework assignment or feedback one week later. On exams, the students who received delayed feedback on their homework outperformed those students who received immediate feedback. In an interview with Craig Roberts for EdSurge, one of the investigators, Andrew Butler (2014), explained his findings: "Essentially a spacing effect—distributing exposure to or practice with material improves long-term retention" (para. 6). Interestingly, the study also found that students preferred immediate feedback and those that received delayed feedback thought they were learning less, even though they outperformed their peers who received immediate feedback. As is often the case when we employ desirable difficulties, it may be especially important to communicate with students about why we are doing what we are doing.

Clariana, Wagner, and Murphy (2000) found that the effectiveness in delays in feedback varied according to the difficulty of the problem. The authors suggest that when dealing with complex problems, it is best to delay feedback because students need the time to process before they receive feedback. In fact, Foerde and Shohamy (2011) used neuroimaging to show that different areas of the brain are activated depending on the type of feedback the learner receives. Those who received immediate feedback showed an activation in a part of the brain that is associated with implicit learning, while those who received delayed feedback showed activation of the hippocampus, which is linked to explicit learning.

While many of us would like to stop grading, that is not, in fact, what delaying feedback is about. It is important to remember that delayed feedback may mean a week rather than an instant. And, of course, any feedback is better than none at all.

Instructional Applications

The following strategies provide instructors with a variety of ways to teach students to think critically, to problem solve, and to learn from their mistakes.

Let Students Discover Their Own Mistakes

It is tempting to correct students instantly; instead, consider letting them continue with a problem until they realize their mistake. For example, if a chemistry class is working a problem together, continue letting them solve the problem, even if they make an error. Wait for them to realize they cannot solve it. Then, have students collaborate to find and correct errors and attempt to solve the problem again.

Generate Knowledge

Ask learners to generate material through an active, creative process. This could involve role-playing, structured debates, puzzles, or scientific study (McDaniel & Butler, 1994). Concept maps are also a great way to have students generate knowledge.

Allow for Confusion

When a concept is difficult, allow students to experience and work their way through their frustration. For example, in a language class, don't help the students by translating. Allow them to feel the confusion and begin to discern the meaning of language. With written assignments, let students know that confusion is part of the process. When students are able to resolve their initial confusion themselves, deep learning can take place. They may feel initial frustration in the writing process, but ultimately they will prevail.

Case Studies or Case-Based Learning

Cases introduce students to challenging real-world problems. They ask students to apply what they have learned in class to devise workable solutions in different contexts.

Send a Problem

For this exercise, instructors divide the class into groups containing four or five students. Each group receives an envelope with a different problem attached. The groups discuss their problem, and at the end of the allotted time, they put their solution into an envelope and give it to another group. The next group tries to solve the problem without looking at the solution in the envelope. After time is called, the groups again pass their problems to a different group. The last group opens their envelope, then analyzes, evaluates, and synthesizes the proposed solutions in order to present their peers with the best approaches and answers.

Team-Based Learning

Team-based learning is a strategy that uses long-term and instructor-assigned groups of five to seven students with diverse skill sets and backgrounds. Students complete assigned readings and homework before taking a quiz in class (to ensure readiness). Immediately afterward, students take the same quiz again with members of their group, this time working on a single answer sheet. Students can appeal answers that their team missed, citing statements in the reading to support their arguments. While most of the class is devoted to small-group activities, the instructor can also build on questions raised during class discussion. Teams are awarded points for working well together. Points are withheld when a team member does not contribute. Learning how to work, interact, and collaborate in a team is essential for success. The instructor's role changes from being the "expert" to facilitating the learning process. For more information on team-based learning see Plank (2011) and Team-Based Learning (n.d.).

Wait for the Answer

Allowing time to think between asking a question and requiring an answer gives students the opportunity to better formulate their answers and, therefore, increases the depth of their answers. It also lets the students know the instructor won't be answering their own questions.

Phone a Friend

To help foster a safe environment where students feel that they can collaborate, give students the option of asking a friend to help them with problems they are writing on the board. This lessens the fear of failure while also creating a collaborative classroom atmosphere.

Make Sure Grading Policies Are in Line With Course Goals

If instructors want students to have a "mastery goal orientation," their classroom policies need to reflect this desire. Consider giving credit for mistakes corrected or partial credit for a concerted effort from the student, even if he or she did not get something right on the first try.

What Is One Thing That Is Wrong?

Ask students if they think their solution is correct. If they do not, have them focus on one wrong thing. If their answer is still not correct, ask them if they can find one more problem with their answer. Continue the process by inviting other students to collaborate in finding a solution.

Fail Nine Times

When engaging in a daunting task, students should be encouraged to embrace failure. In the book *The Five Elements of Effective Thinking*, Burger and Starbird (2012) encourage their readers to think: "In order for me to resolve this issue, I will have to fail nine times, but on the tenth attempt, I will be successful" (p. 49). They claim this frees the learner to try new things and take risks they may not otherwise be willing to take. Let students know they can expect to write many drafts or work at many solutions before they get the right one. This encourages mastery goal orientation.

Share a Personal Story

Students often like hearing about their instructors' struggles, such as a time when they as students have failed or had to work very hard to be successful.

Compare and Contrast in Small Groups

Allow space inside or outside of class for students to compare and contrast their work and help each other elaborate on a solution.

Make Connections

Ask students to make connections between new information and knowledge they may already have. This can be done visually with concept maps, orally in a class discussion, as a think-share-pair activity, or as a writing activity. This process allows the student to activate prior knowledge, and instructors to assess the level of prior knowledge and correct inaccurate perceptions.

Assess Prior Knowledge

Give a pretest, a short writing assignment, or have students create a concept map. Knowing what students do and do not know is essential to scaffolding a project.

Skip or Delay the Online Program

While computer programs can help us grade and can give students immediate feedback, this may make the students feel successful but may not help long-term retention. If possible, set a time delay so there is a lag between student work and reception of feedback.

Make Sure the Students Still Get Feedback

When using online programs, make sure the students don't receive credit for their work until they have clicked a link that shows they have seen the feedback. If students don't internalize their feedback, it won't help them.

Delayed Doesn't Mean Never

Feedback is always better than no feedback. Although a lag time can help long-term retention, if instructors wait too long before giving feedback, students lose interest and the positive outcome of the spacing effect is lost.

Annotated Research Studies

Bell, D. S., Harless, C. E., Higa, J. K., Bjork, E. L, Bjork, R. A, Bazargan, M., & Mangione, C. M. (2008). Knowledge retention after an online tutorial: A randomized educational experiment among resident physicians. *Journal of General Internal Medicine, 23*(8) 1164–1171. doi:10.1007/s11606-008-0604-2

Internal and family medicine residents participated in a study to ascertain the optimal time course for physicians' retention of knowledge. The study concluded that immediate feedback made it seem that the learner was successful, but, in fact, learning needed to be reinforced after one week.

Burger, E., & Starbird, M. (2012). Igniting insights through mistakes. In *The Five Elements of Effective Thinking* (pp. 47–72). Princeton, NJ: Princeton University Press.

This chapter contains thought-provoking and concrete applications on how to fail in order to learn. The applications translate easily into a classroom setting. This reader-friendly chapter focuses on the analysis of mistakes or errors as a source of learning.

Foerde, K., & Shohamy, D. (2011). Feedback timing modulates brain systems for learning in humans. *Journal of Neuroscience, 31*(37) 13157–13167. doi:10.1523/JNEUROSCI.2701-11.2011

The authors use neuroimaging to show that distinct learning takes place in the striatum and the hippocampus. Using functional imaging (MRI), the authors show that individuals activate the striatum when they receive immediate feedback and the hippocampus when they receive delayed feedback. The authors state that their findings "indicate that relatively small changes in the circumstances under which information is learned can shift learning from one brain system to another" (Foerde & Shohamy, 2011, p. 13157).

Hattie, J., & Timperley H. (2007). The power of feedback. *Review of Educational Research, 71*, 81–112. doi:10.3102/003465430298487

Feedback can be powerful in learning, but its effects are not always positive. After a detailed summary of 12 meta-analyses about feedback, the authors devote their time to "the conditions that maximize positive effects of learning"

(Hattie & Timperley, 2007, p. 86). They note, "Students can increase their
effort, particularly when the effort leads to tackling more challenging tasks or
appreciating higher quality experiences rather than just doing 'more' (Hattie
& Timperley, 2007, p. 86). Moreover, it is important when giving feedback
to help students understand three questions: "Where am I going? How am I
going? Where to next?" The study includes a useful section about feedback
and helping students with self-regulation and self-assessment. The article
avers that for tasks that do not require complex thinking, immediate feedback may be more useful, whereas delayed feedback is more useful in assignments that demand students to think and process at deep levels.

Hmelo-Silver, C., Duncan, R., & Chinn, C. (2007). Scaffolding and achievement in
    problem-based and inquiry learning: A response to Kirschner, Sweller, and Clark.
    Educational Psychologist, 42(2), 99–107. Retrieved from http://www.tandfonline
    .com/doi/full/10.1080/00461520701263368?src=recsys

The authors specifically examine problem-based learning and inquiry learning and argue that although this type of learning demands much of the
learner, these learning strategies employ extensive scaffolding, which helps
reduce cognitive load. They offer evidence that demonstrates that problem-
based learning and inquiry learning are effective tools for learning.

Kapur, M. (2012). Productive failure in learning the concept of variance. *Instruc-
    tional Science, 40*(4), 651–672. Retrieved from https://link.springer.com/
    article/10.1007/s11251-012-9209-6

Ninth-grade math students were learning concept of variance. One group of
students was taught with direct instruction, while the other group was taught
with productive failure. The productive failure group was first asked to generate a quantitative index for variance without guidance before receiving
direct instruction on the concept. These students significantly outperformed
the students solely with direct instruction on understanding and transfer.

Kapur, M., & Bielaczyc, K. (2012). Designing for productive failure. *Journal of the
    Learning Sciences, 21*, 45–83.

This study demonstrated that students who were taught to solve math problems without direct instruction (a method termed *productive failure*) outperformed students who were taught by using direct instruction. These
students not only outperformed students on ill-structured problems during
the posttest but also significantly outperformed direct instruction with well-
structured problems. Interestingly, two subsequent studies with students
with significantly lower mathematical ability replicated the findings of the
first study. This article also discusses possible ways to implement productive
failure into course design.

Kirschner, P., Sweller, J., & Clark, R. E. (2010). Why minimal guidance during instruction does not work: An analysis of the failure of constructivist, discovery, problem-based, experiential, and inquiry-based teaching. *Educational Psychologist*, *41*(2), 75–86. Retrieved from http://www.tandfonline.com/doi/abs/10.1207/s15326985ep4102_1?src=recsys

This article argues that although minimal guidance is a popular teaching strategy, it does not help learners without sufficient prior knowledge in a subject matter. The authors state that using minimal guidance for learners goes against what we have learned from the cognitive sciences for the last half century, especially regarding novice-expert learners and cognitive load. The authors specifically talk about problem-based learning, experiential learning, inquiry learning, and constructivist learning as minimally guided approaches.

Mullet, H., Butler, A., Verdun B., & Marsh, E. (2014). Delaying feedback promotes transfer or knowledge despite student preferences to receive feedback immediately. *Journal of Applied Research in Memory and Cognition*, 3, 222–229. doi:10.1016/j.jarmac.2014.05.001

The authors report on a pair of studies they conducted where a group of high-level engineering students received either immediate feedback after turning in online homework or received feedback one week later. The students who received the delayed feedback performed better on similar problems on exams than those who received immediate feedback. However, the students who received delayed feedback believed that they had learned less.

Annotated Resources

Edmonson, A. (2011). Strategies for learning from failure. *Harvard Business Review*. Retrieved from https://hbr.org/2011/04/strategies-for-learning-from-failure

In this article, Edmonson talks about the different types of failures (avoidable, unavoidable, and intelligent). She gives interesting case studies of organizations that have turned failure into positives and gives advice for how to foster a productive environment where team members can learn from failure without being punished.

Huddler, M. (2013). The messy and unpredictable classroom. In *Faculty Focus*. Retrieved from https://www.facultyfocus.com/articles/teaching-and-learning/the-messy-and-unpredictable-classroom/

In this article, Huddler reports what she has learned from colleagues about how to define messy and unpredictable problems and why they are important to learning.

Soderstrom, N. (2015, August 4). Take the path of more resistance. *Mastery, Study Tips*. Retrieved from http://www.lastinglearning.com/2015/08/04/desirable-difficulties-path-of-more-resistance/

Soderstrom summarizes the five desirable difficulties that have received the most research (spacing, interleaving, taking tests, varying learning conditions, and reducing feedback). His paragraph on giving the learner less feedback is of particular interest. He claims that if the learner receives feedback too often, it can become a crutch because the learner needs to be able to correct his or her own mistakes. Soderstrom reminds readers that the "desirable" in desirable difficulties is key, since learners may shut down if they perceive the challenges too difficult to overcome.

Weimer, M. (2011). Mastery and performance orientations. In M. Huddler (Ed.), *Faculty Focus*. Retrieved from https://www.facultyfocus.com/articles/teaching-and-learning/mastery-and-performance-orientations/

In this helpful article, Weimer defines and contrasts *mastery* and *performance orientations*. She discusses the ways instructors can foster mastery orientation in their classes.

Workshop 4.1
Problem-Based Learning

We only think when we are confronted with problems.
—John Dewey (1956)

Complex, real-world problems are used to motivate students to identify and research the concepts and principles they need to know to work through those problems. Students work in small learning teams, bringing together collective skills at acquiring, communication, and integrating information.
—Stanford University, Center for Teaching and Learning website

(Continues)

(Continued)

Problem-based learning (PBL) encourages students to connect disciplinary knowledge to real-world problems—and, in the process, motivates students to learn. PBL is a group-oriented, engaged learning in which students participate in solving complex problems and work together to find a resolution. Because PBL often asks students to focus on open-ended questions, the goal is not to find *a solution,* but instead to find possible solutions—and along the way develop desirable skills, among them the ability to learn from setbacks and to embrace productive failure.

The instructor's role (known as the tutor in PBL) is to enhance learning by guiding students through the learning process, yet it is the students themselves who are expected to construct the learning (Schmidt, Rotgans, & Yew, 2011). In fact, PBL's highly structured format also engages students in the practice of metacognition. For example, before the groups begin their project they must identify (a) what they already know about the topic, (b) what they need to know to solve the problem, and (c) what steps they will have to take to solve the problem. This process demands that students reflect on their own prior knowledge to determine their research needs (Schmidt et al., 2011).

PBL is a research-based method that originated in medical schools. It is now also used widely in undergraduate education. The goals of PBL are to foster effective problem-solving and collaboration skills (Hmelo-Silver, 2004). Studies have demonstrated that PBL boosts long-term retention of knowledge; increases library use, textbook reading, and class attendance; and promotes better study habits (Major & Palmer, 2001; Strobel & van Barneveld, 2009). PBL also encourages studying for meaning rather than simply memorizing facts. Strobel and van Barneveld (2009) found that PBL was more effective than traditional approaches for development of skills, long-term retention, and teacher and student satisfaction. Short-term retention was higher with students who had participated in PBL strategies than with students who studied using more traditional approaches.

Steps for Creating PBL Strategies Within Teams

The following list, adapted from *Study Guides and Strategies* (n.d.), will provide instructors with step-by-step guidelines to use PBL in their classes.

1. Give each team an "ill-structured" problem and ask the small groups to discuss it. Having the team reach a consensus about the issues in each of the following steps is essential.
2. Create lists of what is known about the problem and what strengths and capabilities each team member has.
3. Create a written explanation of the problem based on the group's analysis of what is known and what is still needed to reach a possible solution.
4. List possible solutions, ordering them from strongest to weakest.
5. Choose the best solution.
6. List actions to be taken to solve the problem using a time line.

(Continues)

(Continued)

7. Create a list of what is still needed in order to solve the problems, as well as a list of possible resources. Determine if students will need to work individually or in teams to solve the problem. If the research supports the solution and if there is general agreement, go to step 8. If not, return to step 4. It is imperative that students understand from the beginning they will likely need to return to step four. This is part of the iterative learning process inherent to PBL.
8. Have teams write the solution with supporting documentation outside class and present their findings by summarizing the problem, the process, and the solution.
9. Review the performance.

Annotated Research Studies

Luo, Y. (2017). The influence of problem-based learning on learning effectiveness in students of varying learning abilities within physical education. *Innovations in Education and Teaching International*, 1–11. Retrieved from http://www.tandfonline.com/doi/full/10.1080/14703297.2017.1389288

The goal of this study was to determine if PBL helped development of skill-based learning in physical education. One group of university students received traditional instruction in badminton, while the other group used PBL. The researchers found that the PBL group demonstrated better skills and higher motivation, especially among students who initially showed low ability levels.

Major, C. H., & Palmer, B. (2001). Assessing the effectiveness of problem-based learning in higher education: Lessons from the literature. *Academic Exchange Quarterly, 5*(1), 4–9.

According to this meta-analysis of students in the sciences, there is no significant difference between the knowledge acquired by PBL students and non-PBL students. However, students who learned by solving problems in PBL were more likely to transfer their knowledge to solve new and different problems. Moreover, PBL students were more likely to perceive that their communication skills, sense of responsibility, and critical thinking skills were strong.

Strobel, J., & van Barneveld, A. (2009). When is PBL more effective? A meta-synthesis of meta-analyses comparing PBL to conventional classrooms. *Interdisciplinary Journal of Problem-Based Learning, 3*(1), 44–58.

This meta-analysis compared the effects of PBL to those of traditional forms of instruction. Although traditional approaches were more effective when studying for short-term retention in standardized board exams, PBL was found to be more effective for long-term retention, skill development, class attendance, studying for meaning rather than recall, and satisfaction of students and teachers.

(Continues)

(Continued)

Videos

Short videos that demonstrate PBL classrooms can be found on YouTube.

Erasmus University. (2012, December 13). Erasmus University College—Problem based learning [YouTube video]. Retrieved from http://www.youtube.com/watch?v=ITjZqK_zhcl

Hoffman, C. (2011, February 16). Project-based learning explained by Westminster College [YouTube video]. Retrieved from http://www.youtube.com/watch?v=2KzWu8mQSZo

Online Resources

Bessant, S., Bailey, P., Robinson, Z., Tomkinson, C., Tomkinson, R., Ormerod, R., & Boast, R. (2013). *Problem-based learning: Case study of sustainability education: A toolkit for university educators.* Retrieved from https://www.keele.ac.uk/media/keeleuniversity/group/hybridpbl/PBL_ESD_Case%20Study_Bessant,%20et%20al.%202013.pdf

This source is an online toolkit that helps instructors incorporate PBL into sustainability education.

Lynch, M. (2017, October 13). 7 must-have problem based learning apps, tools, and resources. *The Tech Advocate.* Retrieved from http://www.thetechedvocate.org/7-must-problem-based-learning-apps-tools-resources/

This online blog describes and shares links to seven excellent PBL apps and tools. These resources include strategies such as real-world situations, guidelines for developing questions, and news articles that require students to think critically about the world around them.

5

TEACHING FIRST-YEAR AND AT-RISK STUDENTS TO EMBRACE DESIRABLE DIFFICULTIES

The pool of future college students is rapidly growing more racially and ethnically diverse, putting pressure on policymakers and practitioners to address educational attainment gaps among many traditionally underrepresented populations. . . . The changing demographics of our high school graduating classes will mean greater demand for a college education from students we traditionally have not served well. Higher education must commit to finding innovative, cost-effective ways to prepare those students to succeed in our twenty-first-century global economy.

—David Longanecker (2013)

Chapter 5 explores the issue of increasing the level of difficulty in college courses for students who are already facing significant challenges. We begin our discussion by examining the increased diversity of students in our college classes and the reasons why some students may not be adequately prepared for higher education. We will then examine strategies that may help first-year students and students who are at higher risk of failing become more successful.

In the past 40 years, significant progress has been made in enrolling more students from historically underrepresented groups in U.S. colleges and universities. While enrollment of students in higher education during the past 40 years increased by about 40% overall, minority student enrollment increased by 146%. Hispanic undergraduate enrollment has greatly outpaced other racial/ethnic groups (Kinzie, Gonyea, Shoup, & Kuh, 2008). Students with a wider range of talents and abilities are now coming to college. In addition, about one-third of the students entering college during this time period are first-generation college goers (Kinzie et al., 2008).

Although more students are enrolling in colleges, completion rates vary widely. The U.S. Department of Education (NCES, 2017) reported that 59% of students completed a bachelor's degree by 2015 at the same institution where they started in 2009. The 6-year graduation rate was 62% for females and 56% for males. White and Asian students completed their programs at similar rates—62%—Hispanic and Black students graduated at rates of 46% and 38%, respectively (Tate, 2017).

Lack of Preparation to Succeed

Although increased diversity and higher participation rates in colleges are encouraging, about half of high school graduates are unprepared to succeed academically in college (ACT, 2016). Large numbers of students do not enroll in academically challenging course work in high school, work that is necessary to prepare them for college.

In 2008, the Pell Institute found that 4.5 million low-income, first-generation students were enrolled in postsecondary education; however, only 11% of these first-generation students earned a bachelor's degree after 6 years. Nearly 60% of first-generation students who dropped out did so in their first year (Pell, 2008). Even as recently as 2016, we know that there is a major achievement gap.

> For the past five years, the percentage of first-generation students meeting ACT College Readiness Benchmarks in at least three of the four core subject areas (English, math, reading and science), has remained between 18 percent and 19 percent. More than half of first-generation students—52 percent—met none of the benchmarks. (ACT, 2016)

First-year students may find themselves struggling in college for a variety of reasons. Their high school classes might have been less demanding, so they did not have to spend as much time studying for them. Some of their high school classes likely focused primarily on short-term learning strategies or "teaching to the test" rather than on strategies that involved critical analysis or long-term retention. Their weaker preparation for college can be a significant determent to their success.

Time management is also an issue with first-year students; they find themselves with larger chunks of unscheduled time and are uncertain how to prioritize longer-term projects and papers. Dealing with loneliness and being away from home for an extended period can also have a detrimental effect on students.

Students who are unprepared for the rigors of college or who embark on a new and unfamiliar academic environment may find themselves struggling. Historically underrepresented populations are unfortunately more at risk of failing in college. More of these students find it necessary to work while going to school, which leaves them with less time to study. First-generation college students might also have fewer personal role models from their families and friends. At times, their families are bewildered and unable to offer counsel when they call home for advice when struggling at college. In addition, many historically underrepresented college students report an ongoing nagging feeling that they do not belong in college. Unfortunately, sometimes instructors are not aware of academic deficiencies or personal struggles until it is too late.

Introducing Desirable Difficulties to New and At-Risk Students

When students are new to college or at risk for failing due to a variety of reasons, how do instructors make the learning deliberately difficult without creating too much frustration? In order to avoid becoming discouraged, should these students be protected rather than challenged? While the tendency may be to spoon-feed (Hardman, 2006), serve as helicopter professors, or water down courses, instructors need to focus on increasing structure and support, using high-impact teaching strategies (Kuh, 2008), and communicating high expectations to students.

The importance of including strategies that build confidence and success for all students, and especially historically underrepresented groups, cannot be overstated. Experiences early in the first year establish patterns of behavior that will endure over students' college careers (Kinzie et al., 2008; Schilling & Schilling, 2005). Students should be introduced to academic support resources before students find themselves failing. Giving students the tools to solve problems, write well, participate in class, and study effectively are important skills for students to learn early in the semester.

Rendón (1994) found that focusing on validating and supporting student *effort* rather than on achievement fostered student success, particularly for historically underserved students. These validation activities include calling students by name, providing encouragement and support on student effort, working one-on-one with students, encouraging students to see themselves as strong and capable learners, and providing increased opportunities for students to support and encourage each other in class. Rendón (1994) also found that these actions provided transformational changes in students, accompanied by an increased interest in school and confidence in their ability to learn.

High-impact teaching practices have also been found to be successful in supporting first-year students and underrepresented college students (Fink, 2013; Kuh, 2008). These practices have emerged from the meta-analysis of thousands of research studies that contribute to student learning. These include, but are not limited to, first-year seminars, service-learning, undergraduate research, study abroad, internships, community-based learning, capstone courses and projects, learning communities, early warning systems, peer tutoring and mentoring, active and collaborative learning, frequent low-stakes quizzes, and application of concepts to their lives (Kinzie et al., 2008; Kuh, Kinzie, Buckley, Bridge, & Hayek, 2006; Lam, Srivatsan, Doverspike, Vesalo, & Mawasha, 2005; Stahl, Simpson, & Hayes, 1992; Wang & Grimes, 2001). Amelink (2005) also found increased academic achievement and retention of first-generation college students who reported increased participation in group discussion, presentations, and group projects.

Research comparing traditional lecture courses and active learning courses has consistently found that most students usually perform better in active learning courses than in traditional lecture courses. However, female, minority, and low-income and first-generation students benefit even more from active learning strategies, on average, than White males from more affluent, educated backgrounds. In their study "Getting Under the Hood: How and for Whom Does Increasing Course Structure Work?" Hogan and Eddy (2014) compare student achievement in classes with "low course structure" to those with "higher course structure." They define *low course structure* as "a traditional classroom where students come in, listen to the instructor and leave" (Hogan & Eddy, 2014, p. 454) while higher structured courses are those that included active learning strategies. In the higher structured courses, all demographic groups completed the readings more frequently and spent more time studying. In addition, all demographic groups who participated in active learning strategies achieved higher final grades than did students in the lecture course. Interestingly, the active learning approach worked disproportionately well for African American students—halving the Black-White achievement gap evident in the traditional course. Moreover, the achievement gap was closed between first-generation college students and students from families who attended college.

Unfortunately we also know that traditionally underserved students are the least likely to participate in high-impact practices—due to family circumstances, jobs, and extra responsibilities. There are significant barriers for students who would be most served by these practices to participate in these activities. By examining some of the reasons why practices are so successful we may better be able to serve our unrepresented students in more traditional classes. In Kuh's (2008) speculation of why high-impact practices help bridge the achievement gap, he notes that these practices put students in circumstances where (a) they must interact with faculty and peers about substantive matters over an extended period of time; (b) students get increased performance feedback; (c) students engage in diversity through course design; and (d) the active learning strategies provide opportunities for students to integrate, synthesize, and apply knowledge that is essential to relevant and long-term learning experiences.

By being mindful of the importance of faculty and peer interaction and meaningful and frequent feedback, we may serve these students better even if our courses don't require high-impact practices. For example, at the University of Texas at Austin, psychology professors James W. Pennebaker, Samuel D. Gosling, and Jason Ferrell (2014) used a system called TOWER to deliver personalized in-class quizzes, free online readings, small discussion groups, and live chats to each student's laptop or tablet. They also had daily, short, low-stakes quizzes. Compared with students who took the same course in a more traditional format, the students in the TOWER class participated more in classes, attended class more often, and scored higher on tests. The intervention also reduced the achievement gap by 50% between more and less affluent students.

It is important when instructors are notching up the level of difficulty with students who are at-risk that instructors explain why they are being asked to work so hard, why the topics are spaced and interleaved, why frequent low-stakes quizzes are administered, and why high-impact and active learning strategies are implemented rather than passive teaching strategies. When introducing students to the concept of desirable difficulties, share the research studies with them. Students should also be coached on how to handle, embrace, and learn from setbacks. Remind students that they are capable learners who will struggle during the course, but that is how they will learn more and better. Share with them why the class is not organized to be easy, sequential, and ultimately with less long-term learning. Initially, students will need to be taught how to study effectively and what to do when they experience a setback as they are simultaneously being encouraged to be more independent. In the process, students will learn to be more self-reliant and confident and develop better problem-solving skills. "Once the learner has attained some degree of mastery, ratcheting up the difficulty will help her stay in her 'sweet spot' of engagement" (Paul, 2014, p. 2).

Instructional Strategies

We offer the following strategies in order to help set a welcoming environment in the classroom that encourages students to become engaged early in the semester.

Get to Know Your Students

During the first week of classes, reach out to your students by learning students' names as well as encouraging them to learn the names of their peers. Use name cards on desks, and play name games. Have low-stakes assessments that you have to hand back to students—this will help you know how they are doing and learn their names. Conduct short informal "interviews" with students in your classes before and after class during the start of the semester. The goal is to learn more about students' background and interests, as well as to create the kind of faculty-student bond that is so important to student success (Lewis, Holland, & Kelly, 1992).

Let Students Deliver the "How-to-Succeed-in-This-Course" Messages

In the course syllabus, post comments from former students who can provide effective strategies and approaches.

Set Ground Rules for Attendance and Behavior in Class

Take roll and speak to students the first time they have more than one absence. Show them that you care.

Assess Entering Students' Skills

Ask students to complete a brief reading and writing assignment during the first week of class. This allows instructors to get a baseline assessment of student skills. This strategy will often alert the instructor to students who may need additional support and encouragement during the semester.

Activate Student Buy-In

Ask students to write their personal goals for class on three-inch-by-five-inch cards to invite more buy-in.

Give Low-Stakes Quizzes to Help Students Make Class a Priority

Administering a low-stakes quiz can provide a quick review, a check on basic reading comprehension, a jumpstart for class discussion, and a method to take attendance.

Make Your Expectations Explicit

Stress that the responsibility to learn is the students' and that they must take an active role in the process. That means that students are expected to come to class prepared and ready to learn. In her book, *Teaching Unprepared Students: Success and Retention in Higher Education*, Gabriel (2008) states that it is important to create active learning experiences that will tap into students' prior knowledge and experiences to enhance connections to new material.

Require Students to Interact With the Material

Create interactive strategies for students following each 20 minutes of lecture. For example, an interactive strategy can be a "think-pair-share" to respond to a question posed. This strategy can tap into their previous knowledge and experiences to help enhance their connection to new material.

Assess Student Progress Early

When the first graded low-stakes assignment occurs early in the course, students have an immediate sense of how their studying techniques are working.

Discuss Exam Review Strategies in Class

Give students time to write down their study plans. Following the exam, ask students to revisit and revise those strategies.

Connect New Learning to Old

Help students organize new information into meaningful patterns that connect to their prior knowledge. Create concept maps or outlines to show and reinforce these relationships. Share the research with students on how people learn and explain that learning depends on prior knowledge and experience.

Discuss Learning Strategies

Discuss learning strategies in contexts larger than the course that can be applied to other classes. Encourage students to examine their study habits to see if they are procrastinating. Encourage them to keep a calendar of upcoming assignments.

Assure Students That You Believe They Can Do What Needs to Be Done to Succeed in This Class and in School

Never do for students what they should do for themselves—show them how to be self-reliant, to use resources (Gabriel, 2008).

Encourage Students to Set Up a Support Network

Students need to understand that they are responsible for their own success, but that we all get by with a little help from our friends, family, instructors, and academic coaches. Tell students to seek out people from this support system when they feel discouraged.

Encourage Students to Seek Help

This may be during office hours or from an academic support center.

Tell Students About Summer Bridge Programs

These can be invaluable to incoming first-generation college students and other students who may be underprepared for college. These programs can teach time-management and basic study skills necessary for success in college.

Caring, Sustained Relationships

Students who may be at higher risk of failing in college need relationships with faculty who are trusting and caring. They also need to have opportunities to communicate the complexity, frustrations, and positive aspects of their lives in and out of school. From this base of a caring relationship, instructors can help students form career, personal, and educational goals. While these goals may be challenging, they are often the most motivating, but within reach if the student exercises effort.

Realistic, Hopeful Pathways

Students also need adult help to create realistic pathways. Instructors are reminded to recognize the difficulty of trying a new path. They must both prepare students for obstacles and support them when they run into problems.

Engaging School and Community Settings

Becoming engaged in a setting or group often happens when students have opportunities to receive positive recognition and to make positive contributions. Students also often become more engaged when they can spend time in environments in which teamwork is encouraged and when they get help learning skills that are valuable and helpful in their lives.

Annotated Research Studies

Chasteen, S. (2017). How can I create community in an active classroom, so that students feel encouraged to engage? *PhysPort*. Retrieved from https://www.physport.org/recommendations/Entry.cfm?ID=101221

Chasteen provides suggestions for instructors for engaging apprehensive students in a respectful community of learners in an active classroom. She encourages instructors to start setting the environment on the first day of class by communicating expectations for collaboration. Then students can be engaged in active learning activities throughout the semester. A sense of community and increased class participation is fostered using students' names, humor, and positive body language. Instructors are encouraged to show respect and interest in student ideas by hearing multiple perspectives and not judging the responses. Chasteen's suggestions will help instructors create an atmosphere in which students feel that their input is valued and where they will not be embarrassed if they are wrong.

Elias, M. (2009). The four keys to helping at-risk kids. *Edutopia.* Retrieved from https://www.edutopia.org/strategies-help-at-risk-students

Drawing from recent studies on the topic, Elias has developed four basic principles when teaching at-risk students.

Gross, D., Pietri, E., Anderson, G., Moyanho-Camihort, K., & Graham, M. (2015). Increased preclass preparation underlies student outcome improvement in the flipped classroom. *CBE Lifesciences Education, 14*(4), 1–8.

The investigators compared flipped classrooms and traditional classrooms in physical chemistry classes. Students with the flipped classroom—where students watched their professors lecture online and used class time for problem-solving—scored 12% higher on exams than those students in traditional classes. Female students benefited the most and performed at nearly the same level as their male peers.

Hogan, K., & Eddy, S. (2014). Getting under the hood: How and for whom does increasing course structure work? *CBE Life Science Education, 13*(3), 453–68.

The authors found that courses with active learning components (called higher structured courses) helped close the achievement gap; halving the Black-White achievement gap was evident in the traditional course and completely closed the achievement gap between first-generation college students and students whose families attended college.

Hughes, R., & Pace, C. R. (2003). Using NSSE to study student retention and withdrawal. *Assessment Update, 15*(4), 1–2.

In this article, Hughes and Pace found that students at Humboldt State University who withdrew from classes were less likely to work with classmates on assignments than students who persisted. As a result, instructors created more collaborative learning in first-year courses and organized study groups. Humboldt State also created learning communities to increase opportunities for students to interact with each other.

Pennebaker, J., Gosling, S., & Ferrell, J. (2014). Daily online testing in large classes: Boosting college performance while reducing achievement gaps. *PLoS ONE 8*(11): e79774, 1–8. doi:10.1371/journal.pone.0079774

The investigators used a system called TOWER to deliver online readings, discussion groups, and live chats. They also had daily, short, low-stakes quizzes. Compared with a group of students who took the same course in a more traditional format, the students in the TOWER class participated more in classes, attended class more often, and achieved higher test scores. The TOWER system also reduced the achievement gap by 50% between more and less affluent students.

Workshop 5.1
Community-Based Learning

A form of experiential education where learning occurs through a cycle of action and reflection as students. . . seek to achieve real objectives for the community and deeper understanding and skills for themselves. In the process, students link personal and social development with academic and cognitive development. . . experience enhances understanding; understanding leads to more effective action.
—Janet S. Eyler and Dwight E. Giles Jr. (in Bandy, 2018)

When asking students to engage with difficult tasks or problems, their buy-in is important. We know that students are more likely to be motivated and persevere with a difficult problem when it is relevant to their lives or their careers. Community-based learning (CBL), also known as service-learning, is a powerful strategy to make the classroom come alive. CBL allows learners to gain direct experience with issues that they are grappling with in

(Continues)

(Continued)

their courses. Moreover, research tells us that high-impact practices, such as CBL, are key in helping traditionally underrepresented populations close the achievement gap (Hogan & Eddy, 2014; Pennebaker, Gosling, & Ferrell, 2014). Students who engage in CBL are exposed to diversity through course design and are also given the opportunity to synthesize and apply knowledge that is essential to long-term learning.

It is important to remember that CBL differs from both volunteerism (which focuses on community benefit) and internships (which focus on student benefits). Ideally, CBL should be equally beneficial to the student and the community. CBL works best in the context of a rigorous academic experience. Instructors are encouraged to include a strong academic component that incorporates guiding and challenging the students to process the material and relate it to course content.

Instructors often regard community experiences in the same way they do a traditional text. CBL can function as a primary, supplementary, or optional text. In a traditional course, students are not normally graded on having completed the reading; instead, they are graded on how they demonstrate the knowledge via tests, papers, and presentations. CBL can work in a similar way—students are graded, not for time they spend in the community, but rather for the quality of their academic experience.

Implementing CBL

Instructors who are planning to implement CBL are encouraged to consider the following suggestions:

- *Learning objectives.* Whether creating a new course or revising one, CBL needs to match learning objectives.
- *Role in the course.* Decide what role CBL will play in the course. Will CBL act as a supplemental activity in your course, or will it play a central role? Best practices indicate that CBL is most rewarding when it is a significant component in the course.
- *Community.* Speak with leaders in the community who will be served. Make sure the project will benefit the community in a meaningful way.
- *Time frame.* Allow ample time for planning and executing the project. Generally, it is best to have planned the project and contacted the partnering organization before the semester starts.
- *Student needs.* Students need training and orientation before they begin their project. Also, students need to understand why they are participating in CBL.
- *Paperwork.* Before students start their projects, they may need to have background checks or other paperwork completed. Make sure they are informed about what paperwork they will need and can begin the process early in the semester.
- *Plan for assessment.* Have a clear plan for how students will be assessed in the academic component of the CBL project (Prusinski & Wells, 2015–2016).

(Continues)

(Continued)

Instructional Applications

In what follows we provide examples of CBL in various fields to serve as models for ways it can be incorporated across the disciplines.

Sociology

In a sociology class at Colby College, teams of students met with community leaders, executives, development directors, and boards of nonprofits to get an insider's view of nonprofits. These student teams then took on the challenge of writing fundable grants for their partnering agency. The entire class also acted as a foundation, with a mission statement and parameters for giving grants. Finally, the class reviewed the grant applications and voted on a fundable grant. Through the Learn by Giving and the Sunshine Lady Foundation, the class had $10,000 of real money to be divided among the best proposals. Students were able to not only identify needs in the community and partner with nonprofits but also understand how funding for worthy causes is given or denied. For more information, see Meader (2011).

Research Methods

In a research methods course at Centre College, a sociology professor designed her course to help a local pay-what-you-can café collect data to help them assess if they were making progress in their mission to end food insecurity in Boyle County. Grace Café's mission is to serve clients with respect, regardless of their ability to pay. In 2015, the café applied for city funding but was denied it because they could not provide data to prove they were serving clients who needed food assistance. In this course, the students used what they were learning in research methods to collect data in order for the café to make an appeal to the city commissioners for funding. Students were able to conduct research and analyze data in a real-life setting and do it in a manner that would benefit the community partner. In 2016, Grace Café was awarded funding for the first time, in part, due to their partnership with students in this course.

Environmental Studies

As a capstone experience, students could partner with a local agency involved with environmental issues to determine a question of interest. They would then collect and analyze data and present their findings to the community. The community members themselves would ultimately decide how they wanted to proceed.

Statistics

Students in a mathematical ideas class at Union County College were asked to find a nongovernmental organization (NGO) that needed statistical research. The students were

(Continues)

(Continued)

to assist the NGO in developing a statistical tool, conducting surveys, and analyzing data. This allowed students to use classroom knowledge in a real-world environment (Centre College, n.d.).

Annotated Research Studies

Boyer, E. (1996). The scholarship of engagement. *Bulletin of the American Academy of Arts and Sciences, 1*(1), 18–33.

Boyer (1996) makes a powerful argument for engaged learning, stating that "scholarship has to prove its worth not on its own terms, but in its service to the nation and the world" (p. 18). Excerpts from this article may help students understand why they are being assigned a service project and the project's importance in the classroom.

Bringle, R., Philips, M., & Hudson, M. (2004). *The measure of service learning: Research scales to assess student experiences.* Washington DC: American Psychological Association.

This book provides scales to measure the impact of service-learning. It offers scales to measure things such as critical thinking, moral development, and attitudes.

Campus Compact. (2003). *Introduction to service learning toolkit: Readings and resources for faculty.* Retrieved from http://compact.org/resource-type/syllabi/

This is an invaluable book for those interested in service-learning. It offers information on learning theory and the pedagogy of CBL, as well as practical guidance for those interested in implementing service learning in their classes.

Correia, M., & Bleicher, R. (2008). Making connections to teach reflection. *Michigan Journal of Community Service Learning, 14*(12), 41–49.

The authors discuss ways in which effective reflection can be taught and offer detailed guidelines for teachers to help their students get the most out of the process.

Felten, P., Gilchrist, L. Z., & Darby, A. (2006). Emotion and learning: Feeling our way toward a new theory of reflection in service learning. *Michigan Journal of Community Service Learning, 12*(2), 38–46.

This article stresses the importance of recognizing how dialogue between the emotional and the intellectual form the experience and methodology of service learning.

Hammersley, L. (2013). Community-based service-learning: Partnerships of reciprocal exchange? Asia-Pacific. *Journal of Cooperative Education, 14*(3), 171–184.

This article explores the power dynamics between CBL classes and their partner agencies and brings to light the lack of perspectives from partner agencies in many CBL curricula.

(Continues)

(Continued)

Hatcher, J. A., Bringle, R. G., & Muthiah, R. (2004). Designing effective reflection: What matters to service-learning? *Michigan Journal of Community Service Learning, 11*(1), 38–46.

This study reports on a multi-campus research survey that asked students how emotion and reflection were implemented in their service-learning courses. The results indicated that integrating an academic component with a structured reflective component significantly improved the quality of the course.

Jacoby, B. (Ed.). (1996). *Service-learning in higher education.* San Francisco, CA: Jossey-Bass.

This book of 14 essays analyzes the theoretical approaches to service-learning and provides practical means of implementation.

Prusinski, E., & Wells, S. (2015–2016). *Community based learning at Centre College: Faculty handbook.* Retrieved from http://ctl.centre.edu/assets/cblhandbook.pdf

This handbook is an excellent resource for professors and students who want to engage in service-learning. It also offers examples of CBL across the disciplines and has links to sample syllabi. Although the handbook offers sound pedagogical reasons to implement service-learning, it also offers practical tips—including forms students need to complete and sample contracts with partner organizations.

Videos

The following are brief videos illustrating examples of CBL.

Mount Holyoke College. (2010, March 17). Community-based learning at MHC [YouTube video]. Retrieved from http://www.youtube.com/watch?v=wB5_5X4w_-8

University of Notre Dame, Center for Social Concerns. (2012, October 30). ROLL and CSC community-based learning [YouTube video]. Retrieved from http://www.youtube.com/watch?v=i4YbxoOlCwA

Online Resources

Campus Compact. (n.d.). *Campus Contact.* Retrieved from http://compact.org/resource-type/syllabi/

The website for the national Campus Compact organization has many available resources including sample syllabi, program models, grant opportunities, searchable databases, and more.

(Continues)

(Continued)

Centre College. (n.d.). *Community Based Learning.* Retrieved from http://ctl.centre.edu/community-based-learning.html

Centre College provides an excellent website that includes a handbook on best practices, numerous scholarly articles, and courses with sample syllabi from across the disciplines.

Learning by Giving Foundation (n.d.). *Learning by Giving Foundation.* Retrieved from www.learningbygivingfoundation.org

This foundation promotes "the teaching of effective charitable giving." It supports rigorous, full-credit courses with grants of $10,000 that can be distributed to local nonprofits.

Ryan, M. (2012, June). *Learn and Serve America's Service Learning Clearinghouse.* Retrieved from https://www.ecs.org/clearinghouse/01/02/87/10287.pdf

This database offers syllabi, lesson plans, and project ideas for those who want to include CBL as a component of their course.

University of Michigan. (n.d.). *Michigan Journal of Community Service Learning.* Retrieved from http://ginsberg.umich.edu/mjcsl/

This link gives access to past and present articles from the *Michigan Journal of Community Service Learning.* The journal is peer-reviewed and focuses on the research, theory, pedagogy, and practice of service-learning.

6

NEGOTIATING STUDENT
RESISTANCE

*The biggest obstacle in implementing desirable difficulties
into classroom curricula is likely to be convincing teachers and
students alike that these difficulties are indeed desirable.*

—Jeff Bye (2011)

Chapter 6 addresses student resistance when implementing new pedagogies. Students sometimes use teaching strategies as a scapegoat for other things that trouble them, such as a bad prior experience or what they perceive as an instructor's misbehavior. The chapter includes research on student resistance and introduces strategies to help instructors troubleshoot potential problems in the classroom.

Types of Student Resistance

We ask students to struggle when learning because we hope to lead them to think independently, critically, and even skeptically. However, as we may remember from our own days as students, this is not easy work—and while we want students to learn the material, we do not want our practices to incite rebellion. The good news is that although we may worry about student resistance, scholars in communication studies have noted that resistance can have a positive side. Richmond and McCroskey (1992) observed that resistance in the classroom could be defined as either *constructive* or *destructive*. Seidel and Tanner (2013) suggest that constructive resistance includes

71

"asking challenging questions, offering suggested corrections, helping other students without request, and submitting constructive feedback for instructor improvement" (p. 587). According to a recent study by Nguyen and colleagues (2016), even when students display destructive resistance, it is unlikely to take on the form of an out-and-out revolt. Rather, it takes on more passive forms, those that thoughtful instructors can mitigate. For example, students are more likely to demonstrate resistance by being reluctant to participate or by being off task (and on their phones) during class time.

Interestingly, while professors and students may believe a new or challenging pedagogy fosters resistance, scholars are finding that "little evidence from the research literature appears to support this assumption" (Seidel & Tanner, 2013, p. 587). Felder (2013) comments,

> Whenever I've explored this issue with instructors distressed by it, I have invariably found that the teaching method they were trying was not the real problem. It was either that they were making one or more mistakes in implementing the method, or something else was troubling the students and the method was a convenient scapegoat. (p. 131)

Seidel and Tanner (2013) describe three reasons why students might resist innovative pedagogies:

1. *Fear of "social loafing."* Students may resist group projects because they are afraid their partners will not exert enough effort for a quality product and they will be left holding the bag. Pfaff and Huddleston (2003) note that when students (rightly or wrongly) perceive workload within a group to be unfair, it negatively affects their attitudes.
2. *Students' perception of "misbehaviors" by professors.* Seidel and Tanner (2013) point out that when students are carefully questioned about their negative response to a new pedagogy, it often turns out that their reaction is based not on the pedagogy itself, but rather on the professor's behavior. If professors aren't providing clear expectations or showing up for office hours, for example, especially when they are asking students to work harder, students may resent the professor's lack of availability.
3. *Students' lack of prior experience with the pedagogy.* If students are accustomed to sitting passively in class or "just getting by," asking them to engage with active classroom practices may be out of their comfort zone. Therefore, their negative response may be due to their own background rather than the pedagogy itself. Seidel and Tanner (2013) suggest rather than thinking of student resistance, to think instead of *"student barriers to engaging in active-learning approaches"* (p. 590). They believe that by

using the term *barriers* "we can empathize with the challenges students face in our classrooms" (p. 590). The notion of barriers allows us to collaborate with our students in overcoming hurdles in the teaching and learning process and will help prevent resistant behaviors.

Avoiding Pitfalls

When students productively engage with strategies and materials in our courses, they may be less likely to fall into social loafing. However, as we implement new learning strategies, especially those that ask students to work harder, we can expect to have our own setbacks. Indeed, whenever instructors try new and challenging ways of teaching, implementation bumps are to be expected (Chasteen, 2017). However, with some time and effort, instructors can minimize these.

Examining why students resist and addressing those issues will go a long way toward troubleshooting new pedagogies. For example, as we mentioned earlier, one of the primary reasons students resist new practices is their prior experience. Students often believe that they learn best one way, when, in fact, this perhaps only reflects their comfort level with a particular teaching method. Luckily, informed instructors are able to help students form new beliefs about their own learning (Pintrich, 2003). Metacognitive practices help students become aware of their own strengths and weaknesses as learners. Such reflection can keep learners from making the same mistakes repeatedly. (For specific examples, see "Instructional Applications" in chapter 1.) Moreover, when students reflect on their own learning, it can improve their ability to transfer new information or skills from one discipline to another (Zhao, Wardeska, McGuire, & Cook, 2014).

In order for new pedagogies to succeed, instructors need student buy-in. This process is easier if students believe they are engaging in an activity that is relevant to their life or their careers (Shernoff, 2013). Remind students that when they enter the workforce, they will be asked to deal with unpredictable situations where there may be no easy solutions. Help students stay motivated and focused by showing them how the work in our classes offers the opportunity to practice skills they will need in real-world situations. A simple and potentially inspirational means to demonstrate the importance of the knowledge and skills they are gaining from our class is by inviting a guest speaker to talk about his or her own preparation (and even better if it is a former student!). A more elaborate but powerful way to help students understand how the academy and the world interact is by incorporating community-based learning projects (see Workshop 5.1, Community-Based Learning).

Student Feedback

> *While knowing thyself is useful, it is also useful to know what your students are thinking.*
>
> —Brian Croxall (2012)

Discovering student perceptions early in the term may help instructors negotiate and address student resistance—and it may benefit instructors who are worried about poor course evaluations. Because students believe they have a stake in the process, they often take the opportunity to give midsemester feedback more seriously than they do end-of-the-semester feedback (Nilson, 2016). Instructors then have the opportunity to explain why they are making some requested changes and not others. Instructors who provide reasons for their decisions demonstrate that they are listening to student concerns and can often make a difference in the class climate and learning environment (Lewis, 2001). Moreover, research has found that these evaluations, and the subsequent instructor response, have resulted in significantly higher student evaluations at the end of the term (Cohen, 1980).

In addition to soliciting formative feedback midsemester, some instructors check in with students early and often to find out what is troubling them before reading about it in their formal evaluations. Check-ins also let the instructor know how widespread the problem is and what specific concerns are. Chasteen (2017) suggests using clicker responses or an online survey to identify the source of students' resistance. She believes that if students complain that you're not teaching them anything, "clearly identify the goals of the activity, and include reflective discussion about learning gains afterwards. If students complain that the course is too much work, make sure the learning benefit is clear" (p. 66).

Instructional Applications

The following strategies will help instructors find ways to negotiate student resistance.

Set the Stage!

Minimize student resistance by telling students what you are doing, why you are doing it, and what is in it for them (Felder, 2011).

Give a Group and An Individual Grade

When students do group work, give a group and an individual grade to help ease the fear of social loafing and to keep potential loafers on track.

Help Students Understand Their Goals

Make sure students know that for the group to succeed, individuals have to meet their own goals; make sure group members know the group's overall goal as well as the goals of individual members.

Carefully Structure Groups

According to Chasteen (2017), groups work best with eight or fewer people. Fewer than three does not allow for group diversity, while more than six becomes unwieldly and lengthens the time needed.

Use Peer-Rating Systems

Allow students to rate their peers' contributions in group projects; see details of such peer ratings in Felder and Brent (2016) and Kaufman, Felder, and Fuller (1999).

Address Student Perceptions of Professors' Misbehaviors

These suggestions are offered to address concerns that students may have with their instructors when learning challenging content.

Office Hours. Office Hours. Office Hours.
Especially when trying out new pedagogies, show up for office hours and encourage students to drop by to discuss the class. Remember that students often blame pedagogies for a poor class experience when they actually have complaints about a professor's behavior.

Maintain a Strong Online Presence
Let students know that you are available online and are keeping up with their progress. When they feel instructor encouragement, they are less likely to be frustrated.

Verbal Reminders
Remind students in class that you are willing to meet with them to discuss their concerns. Many students are reluctant to seek out instructors and need to hear that they have multiple ways of seeking help.

Address Past Experiences

Making learning relevant through prior experiences and role-playing can be effective.

Best and Worst Experience
Have students do a quick-write about their best and worst experience with group work. Then have them discuss what made their best experience great and what would have made their worst experience better.

Role-Playing and Advice Giving
Give students three scenarios: one where there is a social loafer in a group; one where a professor seems unavailable; and one where a student has had a bad past experience. Have students help each other (and the instructor) troubleshoot these problems before they occur.

Schedule Midsemester Evaluations

Midterm evaluations can provide valuable feedback to both instructors and students and allow time for course corrections.

What's Working and What Isn't
After the fourth or fifth week of classes, ask students what is working and what improvements need to be made in the course to help them learn more effectively. The response rate will be higher if this evaluation takes place during class. Of course, the evaluations should be anonymous. Students will be able to provide better feedback if they have specific questions to answer, for example, "What do you think is going well in this course?" or "What changes would you like to see to help you learn better?" "What are the changes you need to make in your own habits to help you in the course?" One great model for a midterm evaluation is Eleanor Sayre's (n.d.) "Stop-Go-Change" form. After reading the evaluations, summarize them for the students and discuss plans for implementing or reasons for not implementing their suggestions. Finally, talking to a colleague about these evaluations can also be helpful and can provide another perspective.

Ask Students What They Are Going to Do to Improve Their Own Learning
While midsemester evaluations are important, too often these evaluations reinforce the idea that whether or not students learn is a function of the instructor. One excellent means of doing this is to use a plus/delta chart. There are many variations of the plus/delta, but one that is easy to implement is for instructors to hand out a paper with two columns, one for plus (behavior they want to see continued) and the other for delta (things they would like to see changed). The students first reflect on the positive behavior of the professor and then they list what they see themselves doing well. Next, they reflect on what they find problematic about the class. Afterward, they write what they believe they themselves could be doing to better contribute

to the class. The instructor collects the charts and, after reading them, discusses the results with the students. Thanking the students for their time and input is a great way to begin the discussion. Afterward, the instructor addresses student feedback, letting them know what they will change and what they will not change and why. Two good resources for plus/delta are University of San Francisco (n.d.) and Teach it Slant (n.d.).

Small-Group Instructional Diagnosis

Small-group instructional diagnosis (SGID) "generates feedback from midterm small-group discussion among students about a course. Students offer suggestions to solving problems in instruction for the instructor's consideration" (Clark & Redmond, 1982, p. 2). This technique allows the instructor to gather impartial feedback from students. SGIDs are most effective if they are conducted before the middle of the term because it allows the instructor ample time to make changes. This process requires asking a facilitator to meet with students to collect honest feedback.

Teaching and learning centers can be excellent resources, but colleagues from outside the department or institution can also serve as facilitators. The interviewer should divide students into groups and ask groups to respond to questions such as, "What is working in the class?" "What is not working?" "What suggestions can be offered to improve the class?" "What strategies can you think of to improve your own learning?" The outsider then polls the group as a whole and focuses on consensus and solutions rather than on concerns (Cook-Sather, 2009; Sorenson, 2001). Later, the facilitator discusses students' suggestions and concerns with the instructor. However, for this protocol to work, students must be assured that their anonymity will be preserved. Moreover, make sure a trained facilitator responds to student feedback so that the students know they are heard, while still supporting the instructor. The instructor should be left in the same or better position than before the SGID.

Public Midterm Evaluation Using Google Docs

Midsemester, Croxall (2012) modified settings in a Google Doc to allow students to edit the document and view one another's edits. He then asked them to respond anonymously to two brief prompts during class: "What is working?" and "What could be done better?" He wanted students to know what their peers thought were the strengths and weaknesses of the class. Because the comments were public, students could hold him accountable to respond to them (whether he made changes or not, he had to address the comments). More importantly, this allows students to see the range of responses and lets them understand that what is working for them may not be working for someone else. Croxall (2012) found that students wrote more in response to open-ended questions when typing rather than when writing by hand.

Focus/Advisory Groups

In a large class, the instructor meets every few weeks with 6 to 10 randomly chosen students to talk about how the course is going. In these meetings, it is important that the instructor do more listening than talking. Some colleges and universities have teaching and learning centers that can facilitate these meetings.

Annotated Research Studies

Brownell, S. E., & Tanner, K. D. (2012). Barriers to faculty pedagogical change: Lack of training, time, incentives, and . . . tensions with professional identity? *CBE Life Science Education, 11*, 339–346. Retrieved from http://www.lifescied.org/content/11/4/339.full?ijkey=9e1354a504e56f0223f33fb0a677c708a53f4e48&keytype2=tf_ipsecsha

The authors take a long-term view of how to integrate pedagogical change into the sciences, in particular the life sciences. They first address what they believe are the three major problems (lack of training, time, and incentives) and then go on to discuss ways our professional identities are formed. They believe that before we see radical and *successful* changes in pedagogy, we must broaden the goals of the discipline to include pedagogical training of post-doctoral students, inclusion of research-based pedagogy articles in science journals, and better integration of education sessions into conferences.

Chapman, E. (2003). Alternative approaches to assessing student engagement rates. *Practical Assessment, Research & Evaluation, 8*(13), 1–7.

This article reviews the relevant literature in order to define salient dimensions of student engagement; it then goes on to outline methods that have been used to assess active engagement, with the goal of giving practitioners a broad range of options in order to develop assessments of active learning in their own classrooms. This article differentiates three different types of engagement: cognitive, behavioral, and affective.

Nguyen, K. A., Borrego, M. J., Finelli, C., Shekhar, P., DeMonbrun, R. M., Henderson, C., & Waters, C. (2016). Measuring student response to instructional practices (StRIP) in traditional and active classrooms. In *2016 ASEE annual conference and exposition*. New Orleans, LA. American Society for Engineering Education.

This study explores how students in engineering classes resist active learning strategies. Using a survey instrument called Student Response to Instructional Practices (StRIP) survey, the authors studied how students in traditional classrooms and active-learning classrooms responded to the survey. The authors found that, in general, students were not resistant to active learning strategies.

Seidel, S., & Tanner, K. (2013). Approaches to biology teaching and learning "What if students revolt?"—Considering student resistance: Origins, options, and opportunities for investigation. *CBE—Life Sciences Education, 12,* 586–595.

Although this excellent and well-researched article is geared toward biologists, it is easily applicable across the disciplines. The authors review evidence-based studies to elucidate what is known about student resistance and to discuss strategies to negotiate student resistance. They then go on to evaluate intervention strategies. Their bibliography provides valuable evidence-based resources for those who want to delve further into the research on student resistance and motivation.

Shekhar, P., Demonbrun, M., Borrego, M., Finelli, C., Prince, M., Henderson, C., & Waters, C. (2015). Development of an observation protocol to study undergraduate engineering student resistance to active learning. *International Journal of Engineering Education, 31*(2), 597–609.

Recognizing that there have been few studies on student resistance, these authors present the initial phase of a protocol designed to collect data about instructors' use and students' response to active learning strategies. In this paper, they describe not only a variety of ways that learners resist active learning but also strategies for negotiating student resistance. Their findings, although preliminary, indicate that student resistance is almost always passive (not participating or getting and staying off task) and that students have higher levels of engagement (a) when the professor was transparent about why active learning strategies were being used and (b) when the instructor employed a range of active learning strategies.

Tolman, A. O., & Kremling, J. (Eds.) (2016). *Why students resist learning: A practical model for understanding and helping students,* Sterling, VA: Stylus.

This book describes a theoretical model of student resistance. The contributors to this book describe the reasons why students may resist new pedagogies and offer strategies for integrating new frameworks of learning into our courses. This book includes a chapter authored by students who describe how and why they resist new pedagogies.

Annotated Resources

Felder, R. M. (2007). Sermons for grumpy campers. *Chemical Engineering Education, 41*, 183–184.

In this article, Felder addresses specific student complaints and how to listen and respond to them. His "sermons," or suggested responses, are designed to help students understand the intention behind doing work they would prefer not to do.

Felder, R. M. (2011). Hang in there! Dealing with student resistance to learner-centered teaching. *Chemical Engineering Education, 43*, 131–132.

Felder offers a number of strategies for instructors to consider if they receive poor evaluations after implementing a new teaching strategy. This article has many excellent points for faculty to consider before abandoning their new methodology.

Felder R., & Brent, R. (2016). Common active learning mistakes. *Tomorrow's Professor*. Retrieved from https://tomprof.stanford.edu/posting/1491

Felder and Brent provide an excellent table showing the possible pitfalls of implementing new pedagogies in the classroom. The post goes on to share proactive strategies for avoiding implementation bumps.

University of Colorado, Boulder. (2013). Framing the interactive engagement classroom. *Boulder: Science Education Initiative*. Retrieved from www.colorado.edu/sei/fac-resources/framing.html

Although this invaluable resource is geared toward the sciences, it is easily applicable across the disciplines. It is evidence based and helps guide instructors on important topics such as engaging students productively, helping students become expert learners, assessing student outcomes, and addressing student complaints. We recommend this excellent site to anyone interested in exploring pedagogical innovations.

WORKSHOP ON TEACHING ONLINE COURSES WITH DESIRABLE DIFFICULTIES

The most profound words will remain unread unless you can keep the learner engaged. You can't see their eyes to know if they got it so . . . say it, show it, write it, demo it and link it to an activity.

—James Bates in Domun and Goonesh (2014)

This workshop discusses incorporating desirable difficulties into online courses. It presents resources and strategies to address the unique challenges of the online teaching and learning environment.

About 5.8 million students in the United States were enrolled in online courses in fall 2014, a 3.9% increase from the previous fall according to "Online Report Card: Tracking Online Education in the United States" (Babson Survey Research Group, 2015). In this same year, distance education continued to grow at public and private institutions. Sixty-three percent of chief academic officers at these institutions stated that online learning is critical to their long-term strategy (Friedman, 2016). In the fall of 2017, over 1,000 massive open online courses (MOOCs) offered free university instruction to everyone throughout the world (Open Culture, 2017).

The advance of technology and the development of the Internet have "opened doors to the classroom to the world around us" (Deal, 2002, p. 21). The flexibility of online education has helped many self-motivated and mature students who want to earn a degree while working full-time to support themselves and their families. In contemporary education, teachers and students are able to communicate even if they are separated by distance and time (Deal, 2002; Everson, 2009; Karber, 2003; Li & Irby, 2008).

While more students are gaining access to online education, new and different challenges arise when teaching in a digital environment (Nilson & Goodson, 2017). Prior to considering incorporating desirable difficulties in online courses, we first discuss a few of the embedded challenges of online education.

Motivation

Without the face-to-face interaction in the classroom, learners with low motivation or poor study habits may fall behind without the instructor realizing. Students in online courses may feel lonely or isolated from the instructor and classmates. These students need to be encouraged to find a way to balance their time online with social time elsewhere. In developing working relationships with students, it is recommended that teachers manage communication expectations from the very beginning (Davison, 2005; Gillett-Swan, 2017). Instructors may also need to take more opportunities to initiate spaces for students to participate with their peers in order to enhance their learning experience (Aune, 2002; Singh & Pan, 2004). In addition, it is crucial to allocate weekly assignments and communicate with students on a regular basis (Aune, 2002; Li & Irby, 2008; Lyons, 2004).

Regulation

Many students find the flexibility and freedom to structure their own time to be challenging, as online courses require a lot of time and intensive work (Kumar, 2015). Moreover, assignments and activities that are adapted from a classroom setting to an online environment typically take more time to complete. If no one is holding students accountable for these deadlines, it can be easy to defer completing projects.

Adaptability

While listening and taking notes are often expected in a traditional classroom, online discussions or creating a web page requires action. It takes time for students to become accustomed to course management systems (CMSs) and the methods of computer-based education. Understanding the benefits of e-learning and discussing the advantages and flexibility that online learning offers students may better prepare students for online classes.

Resource Overload

Students may feel overwhelmed with the immense options that online learning provides (Coyner & McCann, 2004; Mesa Community College, 2017). If instructors are able to release the syllabus and materials or website before the course officially starts, students will have an opportunity to preview the course and think carefully about whether it will meet their needs. From the outset, instructors should help students with information literacy, perhaps devising exercises to help students assess if the information they are getting is quality peer-reviewed data.

Technology Proficiency

This is a must for both instructors and students when teaching or taking online courses, as it enables both groups to manage courseware and assignments in an organized manner. Managing computer files and online learning software can seem especially complex for students with beginner-level computer skills. In addition, some students may not have the strong Internet connection that online courses require, and so may become frustrated with that technology (Kumar, 2015). Hands-on or lab work is also difficult to simulate in a virtual classroom.

Assessment Issues

Deal (2002) critiqued how teachers of online programs evaluate student work without meeting them face-to-face. Lyons (2004) added that plagiarism can be a potential problem in online programs. To resolve these issues, Deal (2002) advised the use of clear and precise rubric-based assessment, while Lyons (2004) suggested that students complete a performance-based examination in a nearby test site. Lyons also suggested that teachers be creative with their essay questions to avoid problems with plagiarism.

When students are faced with challenges intrinsic to the delivery system, instructors may ask themselves why would they intentionally put into their course what may seem to students as roadblocks to learning. Remind them that making courses more challenging, especially at the initial phases, produces long-term retention. Online learning lends itself to the process of discovery and interpretation. Moreover, many of the practices we use in regular classes will translate easily to online learning.

Active Learning Opportunities

Active learning is no less important in online learning than it is in the classroom. In fact, it may be easier for students to conduct cooperative group work virtually than face to face. It can be an ideal setting for problem-based learning or team-based learning.

Greater Engagement and Learning

Require all students to participate in discussion threads. Have every student work through different problems and generate ideas and solutions. This may have special benefits to students who are timid, as they may be more likely to post to a discussion and interact with their peers in an online learning process.

Well-Conceived Discussion Questions

Online students have more time to give thoughtful, researched answers, so more can be asked of them. More complex questions can be asked of students that require additional reading and application of course materials.

Spacing and Interleaving

Instructors can be more creative about due dates of projects. Moreover, they have the opportunity to require students to review concepts previously taught without feeling their courses are disorganized. Students can be asked to review concepts from earlier in the course on discussion threads. They can interleave and space (see chapter 2) assignments for increased learning.

Frequent Assessments

Assign frequent assessments. Some of these can be graded online, although research shows that if students have a slight delay in online feedback, their retention is better (Bell et al., 2008).

Intentional and Specific Feedback

Feedback is addressed in detail in chapter 3. Initially, online students may require more feedback to feel connected and less isolated from the instructor. It's also important to note that sending individual and frequent initial e-mails that encourage strong effort helps students feel more connected. Moreover, instructors can express concern with an online student's performance, which will remind students that the instructor is available. A deliberate effort to make contact is especially important in the online environment as students become more independent learners.

Anticipate Setbacks

Encourage students to ask for help when they need it. Establish online office hours and time in Google hangouts. In addition, encourage students to come directly to the instructor during on-campus office hours, if that is possible. Stress that students need to be organized from the beginning of an online course. This organization can include a clean and quiet workplace and keeping track of assignments.

Annotated Research Studies

Frazier, A., & Hooper, C. (2012). From lab to classroom: Implementing desirable difficulties to increase acquisition of foundational knowledge. Retrieved from https://ashleyonteaching.files.wordpress.com/2012/02/lilly-2012-amf-crh.ppsx

The authors share their experiences of implementing desirable difficulties in an online communications course. In a PowerPoint presentation, the authors methodically discuss the challenges and successes of revising an in-class survey course to an online course.

Song, L., Singleton, E., Hill, J., & Kuh, M. (2004). Improving online learning: Student perceptions of useful and challenging characteristics. *The Internet and Higher Education, 7*, 59–70. doi:10.1016/j.iheduc.2003.11.003

The purpose of this study was to gain insight into learners' perceptions of online learning. Seventy-six graduate students were surveyed to identify helpful aspects and perceived challenges based on their online learning experiences. Results of the study indicated that most students agreed that course design, learner motivation, time management, and ease with online technologies affected their success in an online learning experience. Participants indicated technical problems, a perceived lack of sense of community, trouble contacting the instructor when he or she was available, and difficulty in understanding objectives of the online courses as challenges. Suggestions for addressing the challenges include requiring discussion board involvement, encouraging a meeting with the instructor face-to-face or electronically when possible, and giving substantial feedback in the first few weeks of the course.

BIBLIOGRAPHY

Introduction

Bjork, E. L., & Bjork, R. A. (2011). Making things hard on yourself, but in a good way: Creating desirable difficulties to enhance learning. In M. A. Gernsbacher, R. W. Pew, L. M. Hough, & J. R. Pomerantz (Eds.), *Psychology and the real world: Essays illustrating fundamental contributions to society* (pp. 56–64). New York, NY: Worth.

Bjork, R. A. (2017). Creating desirable difficulties to enhance learning. In I. Wallace & L. Kirkman (Eds.), *Best of the best: Progress* (pp. 81–85). Carmarthen, UK: Crown House.

Bjork, R. A., & Allen, T. W. (1970). The spacing effect: Consolidation or differential encoding? *Journal of Verbal Learning and Verbal Behavior, 9*, 567–572.

Bjork, R. A. (1994). Memory and metamemory considerations in the training of human beings. In J. Metcalfe & A. Shimamura (Eds.), *Metacognition: Knowing about knowing* (pp. 185–205). Cambridge, MA: MIT Press.

Bye, J. (2011, May 5). Desirable difficulties in the classroom [Web log post]. *Psychology Today*. Retrieved from http://www.psychologytoday.com/blog/all-about-addiction/201105/desirable-difficulties-in-the-classroom

Carpenter, S. K., Cepeda N. J., Rohrer D., Kang S. H., & Pashler H. (2012). Using spacing to enhance diverse forms of learning: Review of recent research and implications for instruction. *Education Psychology, 24*, 369–378. doi:10.1007/s10648-012-9205-z

Cepeda, N., Coburn, N., Rohrer, D., Wixted, J., Mozer, M., & Pashler, H. (2009). Optimizing distributed practice: Theoretical analysis and practical implications. *Experimental Psychology, 56*(4), 236–246. doi:10.1027/1618-3169.56.4.236

Diemand-Yauman, C., Oppenheimer, D., & Vaughan, E. (2011). Fortune favors the bold (and the italicized): Effects of disfluency on educational outcomes. *Cognition, 118*(1), 111–115. doi:10.1016/j.cognition.2010.09.012

Duckworth, A. (2016). *Grit: The power of passion and perseverance.* New York, NY: Scribner.

Dweck, C. S. (2006). *Mindset: The new psychology of success.* New York, NY: Random House.

Fani, T., & Ghaemi, F. (2011). Implications of Vygotsky's zone of proximal development (ZPD) in teacher education: ZPTD and self-scaffolding. *Procedia—Social and Behavioral Sciences, 29*, 1549–1554. doi:10.1016/j.sbspro.2011.11.396

Felder, R. M. (2011). Hang in there! Dealing with student resistance to learner-centered teaching. *Chemical Engineering Education, 43*, 131–132.

Gladwell, M. (2013). *David and Goliath: Underdogs, misfits, and the art of battling giants.* New York City, New York: Little, Brown and Company.

Hattie, J., & Timperley, H. (2007). The power of feedback. *Review of Educational Research, 71,* 81–112. doi:10.3102/003465430298487

Kapur, M. (2014). Comparing learning from productive failure and vicarious failure. *Journal of Teacher Education, 23*(4), 651–677.

Kapur, M., & Bielaczyc, K. (2012). Designing for productive failure. *Journal of the Learning Sciences, 21,* 45–83.

Karpicke, J., & Blunt, J. (2011). Retrieval practice produces more learning than elaborative studying with concept mapping. *Science, 331*(6018), 772–775. doi:10.1126/science.1199327

McDaniel, M. A., & Butler, A. C. (2011). A contextual framework for understanding when difficulties are desirable. In A. Benjamin (Ed.), *Successful remembering and successful forgetting: A Festschrift in honor of Robert A. Bjork* (pp. 175–199). New York, NY: Taylor & Francis.

McNamara, D. S., Kintsch, E., Songer, N. B., & Kintsch, W. (1996). Are good texts always better? Interactions of text coherence, background knowledge, and levels of understanding in learning from text. *Cognition and Instruction, 14,* 1–43.

Metcalfe J. (2009). Metacognitive judgments and control of study. *Current Directions in Psychological Science, 18*(3), 159–163. doi:10.1111/j.1467-8721.2009 .01628.x

Roediger, H., & Karpicke, J. D. (2006). Test-enhanced learning: Taking memory tests improves long-term retention. *Psychological Science, 17*(3), 249–255.

Rohrer, D., Dedrick, R. F., & Stershic, S. (2015). Interleaved practice improves mathematics learning. *Journal of Educational Psychology, 107*(3), 900–908. doi:10.1037/edu0000001

Rohrer, D., & Taylor, K. (2007). The shuffling of mathematics practice problems improves learning. *Instructional Science, 35,* 481–498.

Smith, S. M., Glenberg, A., & Bjork, R. A. (1978). *Memory & Cognition, 6,* 342. https://doi.org/10.3758/BF03197465

Vygotsky, L. S. (1978*). Mind in society: The development of higher psychological processes.* Boston, MA: Harvard University Press.

Chapter 1

Aronson, J., Fried, C., & Good, C. (2001). Reducing the effects of stereotype threat on African American college students by shaping theories of intelligence. *Journal of Experimental Social Psychology, 38*(2), 113–125. doi:10.1006/jesp.2001.1491

Barseghian, T. (2013, September 12). Why teaching mindfulness benefits students' learning. *Mind/Shift.* Retrieved from https://ww2.kqed.org/mindshift/2013/09/12/why-teaching-mindfulness-benefits-students-learning/

Bennett, J. (2017, June 24). On campus, failure is on the syllabus. *New York Times*. Retrieved from https://www.nytimes.com/2017/06/24/fashion/fear-of-failure.html

Blackwell, L., Dweck, C., & Trzesniewski, K. (2007). Achievement across the adolescent transition: A longitudinal study and an intervention. *Child Development, 78*(1), 246–263.

Bureau of Study Counsel. (n.d.). *Success-failure project: Exploring success, failure and resilience.* Harvard University. Retrieved from https://successfailureproject.bsc.harvard.edu/

Colvin, G. (2008). *Talent is overrated: What really separates world-class performers from everybody else.* London, UK: Portfolio.

Duckworth, A. (2013). *The power of passion and perseverance* [TED Talk]. Retrieved from https://www.ted.com/talks/angela_lee_duckworth_grit_the_power_of_passion_and_perseverance

Duckworth, A. (2016). *Grit: The power of passion and perseverance.* New York, NY: Scribner.

Duckworth, A. L., Quinn, P., & Seligman, M. (2009). Positive predictors of teacher effectiveness. *Journal of Positive Psychology, 4*(6), 540–547.

Dweck, C. S. (2006). *Mindset: The new psychology of success.* New York, NY: Random House.

Dweck, C. (2014). The power believing you can improve. TED Talk retrieved from https://www.ted.com/talks/carol_dweck_the_power_of_believing_that_you_can_improve

Dweck, C., Walton, G., & Cohen, G. (2014) *Academic tenacity: Mindsets and skills that promote long-term learning.* Bill & Melinda Gates Foundation. Retrieved from https://ed.stanford.edu/sites/default/files/manual/dweck-walton-cohen-2014.pdf

Engber, D. (2016, May 8). Is "grit" really the key to success? *Slate.* Retrieved from http://www.slate.com/articles/health_and_science/cover_story/2016/05/angela_duckworth_says_grit_is_the_key_to_success_in_work_and_life_is_this.html

Harvard University. (2017). *Resilience Consortium home page.* Retrieved from https://resilienceconsortium.bsc.harvard.edu/

Heckman, J. J., Stixrud, J., & Urzua, S. (2006). The effects of cognitive and noncognitive abilities on labor market outcomes and social behavior. *Journal of Labor Economics, 24*, 411–482.

Hulleman, C. S., & Harackiewicz, J. M. (2009). Making education relevant: Increasing interest and performance in high school science classes. *Science, 326*(5958), 1410–1412.

McDaniel, M. A., & Butler, A. C. (2011). A contextual framework for understanding when difficulties are desirable. In A. S. Benjamin (Ed.), *Successful remembering and successful forgetting: A festschrift in honor of Robert A. Bjork* (pp. 175-198). New York, NY, US: Psychology Press.

Molden, D. C., & Dweck, C. S. (2006). Finding "meaning" in psychology: A lay theories approach to self-regulation, social perception, and social development. *American Psychologist, 61*(3), 192–203. doi:10.1037/0003-066X.61.3.192

Mueller, C. M., & Dweck, C. S. (1998). Praise for intelligence can undermine children's motivation and performance. *Journal of Personality and Social Psychology*, *75*, 33.

Paunesku, D., Walton, G. M., Romero, C. L., Smith, E. N., Yeager, D. S., & Dweck, C. S. (2015). Mindset interventions are a scalable treatment for academic underachievement. *Psychological Science, 26*(6), 784–793.

Princeton University. (n.d.). *Princeton perspective project.* Retrieved from https://perspective.princeton.edu/about-ppp/about-ppp

Robertson-Craft, C., & Duckworth, A. L. (2014). True grit: Trait-level perseverance and passion for long-term goals predicts effectiveness and retention among novice teachers, *Teachers College Record,* 116(3), 1–27. Retrieved from http://www.tcrecord.org/Content.asp?ContentId=17352

Robinson, K. (2006). *Do schools kill creativity?* [TED Talk]. Retrieved from https://www.ted.com/talks/ken_robinson_says_schools_kill_creativity

Stephens, N. M., Hamedani, M. Y. G., & Destin, M. (2014). Closing the social-class achievement gap: A difference-education intervention improves first-generation students' academic performance and all students' college transition. *Psychological Science, 25*(4), 943–953. doi:10.1177/0956797613518349

University of Pennsylvania. (n.d.). *Penn Faces: The Resilience Project.* Retrieved from https://perspective.princeton.edu/about-ppp/about-ppp

Walton, G. M., & Cohen, G. L. (2007). A question of belonging: Race, social fit, and achievement. *Journal of Personality and Social Psychology, 92*, 82–96. doi:10.1037/0022-3514.92.1.82

Yan, V. X., Bjork, E. L., & Bjork, R. A. (2016). On the difficulty of mending metacognitive illusions: A priori theories, fluency effects, and misattributions of the interleaving benefit. *Journal of Experimental Psychology: General, 145*, 918–933.

Yeager, D. S., & Dweck, C. S. (2012). Mindsets that promote resilience: When students believe that personal characteristics can be developed. *Educational Psychologist, 47*(4), 302–314.

Chapter 2

Adesope, O., Tervisan, A., & Sundararajan, N. (2017). Rethinking the use of tests: A meta-analysis of practice testing. *Review of Educational Research, 87*(3), 659–701. doi:10.3102/0034654316689306

Anderson, L. W., & Krathwohl, D. R. (Eds.). (2001). *A taxonomy for learning, teaching, and assessing: A revision of* Bloom's Taxonomy of Educational Objectives (Complete edition). New York, NY: Longman.

Atkinson, R. C., & Shiffrin, R. M. (1968). Human memory: A proposed system and its control processes. In K. W. Spence & J. T. Spence (Eds.), *The psychology of learning and motivation* (Vol. 2) (pp. 89–195). New York, NY: Academic Press.

Baddeley, A. D. (1986). *Working memory* (Oxford Psychology Series No. 11). Oxford, UK: Clarendon.

Baddeley, A., & Longman, D. J. A. (1978). The influence of length and frequency on training sessions on the rate of learning to type. *Ergonomics, 21,* 627–635.

Baume, D., & Baume, C. (2008). *Powerful ideas in teaching and learning.* Wheatley, UK: Oxford Brookes University.

Berkley, E. (2010). *Student engagement techniques: A handbook for college faculty.* San Francisco, CA: Jossey-Bass.

Bertsch, S., Pesta, B., Wiscott, B., & McDaniel, M. (2007). The generation effect: A meta-analytic review. *Memory & Cognition, 35*(2), 201–210.

Bjork, E. L., & Bjork, R. A. (2011). Making things hard on yourself, but in a good way: Creating desirable difficulties to enhance learning. In M. A. Gernsbacher, R. W. Pew, L. M. Hough, & J. R. Pomerantz (Eds.), *Psychology and the real world: Essays illustrating fundamental contributions to society* (pp. 56–64). New York, NY: Worth.

Bjork, R. A. (2011). On the symbiosis of learning, remembering, and forgetting. In A. S. Benjamin (Ed.), *Successful remembering and successful forgetting: A Festschrift in honor of Robert A. Bjork* (pp. 1–22). London, UK: Psychology Press.

Black, P., Harrison, C., Lee, C., Marshall, B., & William, D. (2003). *Assessment for learning: Putting it into practice.* Buckingham, UK: Open University Press. Retrieved from http://www.canterbury.ac.uk/education/protected/ppss/docs/gtc-afl.pdf

Black, P., Harrison, C., Lee, C., Marshall, B., & William, D. (2004). Working inside the black box: Assessment for learning in the classroom. *Phi Delta Kappan, 86,* 1–8.

Bloom, B., & Krathwohl, D. (1956). *Taxonomy of educational objectives: The classification of educational goals, by a committee of college and university examiners. Handbook 1: Cognitive domain.* New York, NY: Longmans.

Brown, P. C., Roediger, H. L., & McDaniel, M. A. (2014). *Make it stick: The science of successful learning.* Cambridge, MA: Harvard University Press.

Bui, D., & McDaniel, M. (2015, June). Enhancing learning during lecture note-taking using outlines and illustrative diagrams. *Journal of Applied Research in Memory and Cognition, 4*(2), 129–135.

Butler, A. (2010). Repeated testing produces superior transfer of learning relative to repeated studying. *Journal of Experimental Psychology: Learning, Memory, and Cognition, 36*(5), 1118–1133.

Cram. (n.d.). *Create a new flashcard set.* Retrieved from http://www.cram.com/flashcards/create

Dempster, F. (1990). The spacing effect: Research and practice. *Journal of Research and Development in Education, 23*(2), 97–101.

DeWinstanley, P. A., & Bjork, E. L. (2004). Processing strategies and the generation effect: Implications for making a better reader. *Memory and Cognition, 32*(6), 945–955. Retrieved from https://www.ncbi.nlm.nih.gov/pubmed/15673182

Dunlosky, J., Rawson, K., Marsh, E., Nathan, M., & Willingham, D. (2013). Improving students' learning with effective learning techniques: Promising directions from cognitive and educational psychology. *Psychological Science in the Public Interest, 14*(1), 4–58.

Ginns, P. (2005). Meta-analysis of the modality effect. *Learning and Instruction, 15,* 313–331.

Hodges, D. (2010). Can neuroscience help us do a better job of teaching music? *General Music Today, 23*(3), 3–12.

Jacoby, J., & Chestnut, R. (1978). *Brand loyalty, measurement and management.* New York, NY: John Wiley & Sons.

Karpicke, J. D. (2016). A powerful way to improve learning and memory. *APA Psychological Science Agenda.* Retrieved from http://www.apa.org/science/about/psa/2016/06/learning-memory.aspx

Karpicke, J., & Blunt, J. (2011). Retrieval practice produces more learning than elaborative studying with concept mapping. *Science, 331*(6018), 772–775. doi:10.1126/science.1199327

Kember, D., Ho, A., & Hong, C. (2008). The importance of establishing relevance in motivating student learning. *Active Learning in Higher Education, 9*(3), 249–263.

Kornell, N., Hays, M. J., & Bjork, R. A. (2009). Unsuccessful retrieval attempts enhance subsequent learning, *Journal of Experimental Psychology: Learning, Memory, and Cognition, 35*(4), 989–998. Retrieved from https://bjorklab.psych.ucla.edu/wp-content/uploads/sites/13/2016/07/Kornell_Hays_Bjork_2009_JEP-LMC.pdf

McDaniel, M. A., & Butler, A. C. (2011). A contextual framework for understanding when difficulties are desirable. In A. S. Benjamin (Ed.), *Successful remembering and successful forgetting: A Festschrift in honor of Robert A. Bjork* (pp. 175–198). London, UK: Psychology Press.

McDaniel, M. A., Waddill, P. J., & Einstein, G. O. (1988). A contextual account of the generation effect: A three-factor theory. *Journal of Memory and Language, 27*(5), 521–536.

Medina, J. (2014). *Brain rules* (2nd ed.). Seattle, WA: Pear Press.

Nilson, L. B. (2016). *Teaching at its best: A research-based resource for college instructors* (4th ed.) (pp. 243–245). San Francisco, CA: Jossey-Bass.

Pieters, R., & Wedel, M. (2005). Attention capture and transfer in advertising: Brand, pictorial, and text-size effects. *Journal of Marketing, 68*(2), 36–50. doi:10.1509/jmkg.68.2.36.27794

Prince, M. (2004). Does active learning work? A review of the research. *Journal of Engineering Education, 93*(3), 223–231.

Quizlet (n.d.). *Create a new study set.* Retrieved from https://quizlet.com/create-set

Rees, E. (2016) *Science of learning: Repeated retrieval yields retention.* Lessonly. Retrieved from https://www.lessonly.com/blog/science-of-retrieval/

Richards, B., & Frankland, P. W. (2017). The persistence and transience of memory. *Neuron, 94*(6), 1071–1084.

Roediger, H., & Karpicke, J. D. (2006). Test-enhanced learning: Taking memory tests improves long-term retention. *Psychological Science, 17*(3), 249–255.

Seekers, M. J., Bonasia, K., St-Laurent, M., Pishdadian, S., Winocur, G., Grady, C. & Moscovitch, M. (2016). Recovering and preventing loss of detailed memory: Differential rates of forgetting for detail types in episodic memory. *Learning and Memory, 23*(2) 72–82. doi:10.1101/lm.039057.115

Slamecka, N., & Graf, P. (1978). Generation effect: Delineation of a phenomenon. *Journal of Experimental Psychology, Human Learning and Memory, 4*(6), 592–604.

Stenberg, G. (2006). Conceptual and perceptual factors in the picture superiority effect. *European Journal of Cognitive Psychology, 18*(6), 813–847. doi:10.1080/09541440500412361

Svinicki, M. (2004). *Learning and motivation in the post-secondary classroom.* San Francisco, CA: Jossey-Bass.

Terada, Y. (2017). Why students forget—and what you can do about it. *Edutopia.* Retrieved from https://www.edutopia.org/article/why-students-forget-and-what-you-can-do-about-it

Terada, S., Sakurai, Y., Nakahara, H., & Fujisawa, S. (2017). Temporal and rate coding for discrete event sequences in the hippocampus. *Neuron, 94*(6), 1248–1262. doi:10.1016/j.neuron.2017.05.024

Van Blerkom, D., Van Blerkom, M., & Bertsch, S. (2006). Study strategies and generative learning: What works? *Journal of College Reading and Learning, 37*(1), 7–18. Retrieved from https://files.eric.ed.gov/fulltext/EJ747769.pdf

Willingham, D. (2009). *Why don't students like school?: A cognitive scientist answers questions about how the mind works and what it means for the classroom.* San Francisco, CA: Jossey-Bass.

Wittrock, M. C., & Alesandrini, K. (1990). Generation of summaries and analogies and analytic and holistic abilities, *American Educational Research Journal, 27*(3) 489–502.

Yan, V. X., Bjork, E. L., & Bjork, R. A. (2016). On the difficulty of mending metacognitive illusions: *A priori* theories, fluency effects, and misattributions of the interleaving benefit. *Journal of Experimental Psychology: General, 145,* 918–933. Retrieved from https://drive.google.com/file/d/0B1VOOiLjF_ytU2UtOFpuMW9HMjQ/view

Zull, J. E. (2002). *The art of changing the brain: Enriching the practice of teaching by exploring the biology of learning.* Sterling, VA: Stylus.

Chapter 3

Bahrick, H. P. (1979). Maintenance of knowledge: Questions about memory we forgot to ask. *Journal of Experimental Psychology: General, 108,* 296–308.

Benjamin, A. S., & Tullis, J. (2010). What makes distributed practice effective? *Cognitive Psychology, 61*(3), 228–247. doi:10.1016/j.cogpsych.2010.05.004

Bird, S. (2010). Effects of distributed practice on the acquisition of second language English syntax. *Applied PsychoLinguistics, 31,* 635–650.

Bjork, E. L., & Bjork, R. A. (2011). Making things hard on yourself, but in a good way: Creating desirable difficulties to enhance learning. In M. A. Gernsbacher, R. W. Pew, L. M. Hough, & J. R. Pomerantz (Eds.), *Psychology and the real world: Essays illustrating fundamental contributions to society* (pp. 56–64). New York, NY: Worth.

Bjork, R. A. (1994). Memory and metamemory considerations in the training of human beings. In J. Metcalfe & A. Shimamura, (Eds.), *Metacognition: Knowing about knowing* (pp. 185–205). Cambridge, MA: MIT Press.

Bjork, R. A. (2017). Creating desirable difficulties to enhance learning. In I. Wallace & L. Kirkman (Eds.), *Best of the best: Progress* (pp. 81–85). Carmarthen, UK: Crown House.

Bjork, R. A., & Allen, T. W. (1970). The spacing effect: Consolidation or differential encoding? *Journal of Verbal Learning and Verbal Behavior, 9*, 567–572.

Bjork, R. A., & Bjork, E. L. (1992). A new theory of disuse and an old theory of stimulus fluctuation. In A. Healy, S. Kosslyn, & R. Shiffrin (Eds.), *Learning processes to cognitive processes: Essays in honor of William K. Estes* (Vol. 2) (pp. 35–67). Hillsdale, NJ: Erlbaum.

Carpenter, S., Cepeda, N., Roher, D., Kang, S., & Pashler, H. (2012). Using spacing to enhance diverse forms of learning: Review of recent research and implications for instruction. *Education Psychology Review, 24,* 369–378. Retrieved from https://public.psych.iastate.edu/shacarp/Carpenter_et_al_2012.pdf

Carpenter, S. K., & DeLosh, E. L. (2005). Application of the testing and spacing effects to name-learning. *Applied Cognitive Psychology, 19*, 619–636.

Carson, L., & Wiegand, R. (1979). Motor schema formation and retention in young children. *Journal of Motor Behavior, 11*(4) 247–51. doi:10.1080/00222895.1979.10735193

Cepeda, N.J., Coburn, N., Rohrer, D., Wixted, J., Mozer, M., & Pashler, H. (2009). Optimizing distributed practice: Theoretical analysis and practical implications. *Experimental Psychology, 56*(4), 236–246. doi:10.1027/1618-3169.56.4.236

Cepeda, N. J., Pashler, H. Vul, E., Wixted, J. T., & Rohrer, D. (2009). Distributed practice in verbal recall tasks: A review and quantitative synthesis. *Psychological Bulletin, 132*(3), 354–380.

Cepeda, N. J., Vul, E., Rohrer, D., Wixted, J. T., & Pashler, H. (2008). Spacing effects in learning a temporal ridgeline of optimal retention. *Psychological Science, 19*(11), 1095–1102.

Cull, W. L. (2000). Untangling the benefits of multiple study opportunities and repeated testing for cued recall. *Applied Cognitive Psychology, 14*, 215–235.

Cull, W. L., Shaughnessy, J. J., & Zechmeister, E. B. (1996). Expanding understanding of the expanding-pattern-of-retrieval mnemonic: Toward confidence in applicability. *Journal of Experimental Psychology: Applied, 2*(4), 365–378. doi:10.1037/1076-898X.2.4.365

Dempster, F. N. (1988). The spacing effect: A case study in the failure to apply the results of psychological research. *American Psychologist, 43*(8), 627–634.

Ebbinghaus, H. E. (1964). *Memory: A contribution to experimental psychology*. New York, NY: Dover.

Francisco, A. (2015). Ask the cognitive scientist: Distributed practice. *Digital promise: Accelerating innovation in education*. Retrieved from http://digitalpromise.org/2015/01/22/ask-the-cognitive-scientist-distributed-practice/

Goode, S., & Magill, R. (1986). Contextual interference effects in learning three badminton serves. *Research Quarterly for Exercise and Sport, 57*(4), 308–314. doi: 10.1080/02701367.1986.10608091

Hatala, R., Brooks, L., & Norman, G. (2003). Practice makes perfect: The critical role of mixed practice in the acquisition of ECG interpretation Skills. *Advances in Health Sciences Education, 8*(1), 17–26.

Hattie, J. (2008). *Visible learning: A synthesis of over 800 meta-analyses relating to achievement.* New York, NY: Routledge.

Hser, Y., & Wickens, T. D. (1989). The effects of the spacing of test trials and study trials in paired-association learning. *Educational Psychology, 9*(2), 99–120. doi:10.1080/0144341890090202

James, W. (1899). *Talks to teachers on psychology: And to students on some of life's ideals.* New York, NY: Henry Holt.

Jenkins, J. (2013). *Interleaved practice: A secret enhanced learning technique.* Retrieved from http://j2jenkins.com/2013/04/29/interleaved-practice-a-secret-enhanced-learning-technique/

Kang, S. H. (2016). Spaced repetition promotes efficient and effective learning policy implications for instruction. *Policy Insights from the Behavioral and Brain Sciences, 3*(1), 12–19. doi:10.1177/2372732215624708

Kornell, N. (2009). Optimising learning using flashcards: Spacing is more effective than cramming. *Applied Cognitive Psychology, 23*, 1297–1317. doi:10.1002/acp.1537

Kornell, N., & Bjork R. A. (2008). Learning concepts and categories: Is spacing the "enemy of induction"? *Psychological Science, 19*, 585–592. doi:10.1111/j.1467-9280.2008.02127.x

Kuh, G. D. (2008). *High-impact educational practices: What they are, who has access to them, and why they matter.* Washington DC: Association of American Colleges & Universities.

Küpper-Tetzel, C. E., Kapler, I. V., & Wiseheart, M. (2014). Contracting, equal, and expanding learning schedules: The optimal distribution of learning sessions depends on retention interval. *Memory & Cognition, 42*(5), 729–741.

Landauer, T. K., & Bjork, R. A. (1978). Optimum rehearsal patterns and name learning. In M. Gruneberg, P. E. Morris, & R. N. Sykes (Eds.), *Practical aspects of memory* (pp. 625–632). London, UK: Academic Press.

Mozer, M. C., Pashler, H., Cepeda, N., Lindsey, R., & Vul, E. (2009, Dec. 7–10). Predicting the optimal spacing of study: A multiscale context model of memory. In Y. Bengio, D. Schuurmans, J. Lafferty, C. K. I. Williams, & A. Culotta (Eds.), *Proceedings of the 22nd International Conference on Advances in neural information processing systems.* Paper presented at Vancouver, British Columbia, Canada (pp. 1321–1329). La Jolla, CA: NIPS.

Pan, S. (2015, August). The interleaving effect: Mixing it up boosts learning. *Scientific American.* Retrieved from https://www.scientificamerican.com/article/the-interleaving-effect-mixing-it-up-boosts-learning/

Rawson, K. A., & Dunlosky, J. (2011). Optimizing schedules of retrieval practice for durable and efficient learning: How much is enough? *Journal of Experimental Psychology: General, 140*(3), 283.

Rawson, K. A., Dunlosky, J., & Sciartelli, S. M. (2013). The power of successive relearning: Improving performance on course exams and long-term retention. *Educational Psychology Review, 25*(4), 523–548.

Roediger, H. L., & Karpicke, J. D. (2011). Intricacies of spaced retrieval: A resolution. In A. S. Benjamin (Ed.), *Successful remembering and successful forgetting: Essays in honor of Robert A. Bjork* (pp. 23–47). New York, NY: Psychology Press.

Rohrer, D., Dedrick, R. F., & Burgess, K. (2014). The benefit of interleaved mathematics practice is not limited to superficially similar kinds of problems. *Psychonomic Bulletin & Review, 21,* 1323–1330.

Rohrer, D., Dedrick, R. F., & Stershic, S. (2015). Interleaved practice improves mathematics learning. *Journal of Educational Psychology, 107*(3), 900–908. doi:10.1037/edu0000001

Rohrer, D., & Taylor, K. (2006). The effects of overlearning and distributed practice on the retention of mathematics knowledge. *Applied Cognitive Psychology, 20,* 1209–1224.

Rohrer, D., & Taylor, K. (2007). The shuffling of mathematics problems improves learning. *Instructional Science, 35,* 481–498. doi:10.1007/s11251-007-9015-8

Yan, V. X., Bjork, E. L., & Bjork, R. A. (2016). On the difficulty of mending metacognitive illusions: A priori theories, fluency effects, and misattributions of the interleaving benefit. *Journal of Experimental Psychology: General,* 145, 918–933.

Chapter 4

Ames, C., & Archer, J. (1988). Achievement goals in the classroom: Students' learning strategies and motivation processes. *Journal of Educational Psychology, 80*(3), 260–267. doi:10.1037/0022-0663.80.3.260

Bell, D. S., Harless, C. E., Higa, J. K., Bjork, E. L., Bjork, R. A., Bazargan, M., & Mangione, C. M. (2008). Knowledge retention after an online tutorial: A randomized educational experiment among resident physicians. *Journal of General Internal Medicine, 23*(8) 1164–1171. doi:10.1007/s11606-008-0604-2

Bjork, E. L., & Bjork, R. A. (2014). Making things hard on yourself, but in a good way: Creating desirable difficulties to enhance learning. In M. A. Gernsbacher & J. Pomerantz (Eds.), *Psychology and the real world: Essays illustrating fundamental contributions to society* (2nd ed.) (pp. 59–68). New York, NY: Worth.

Brown, P. C., Roediger, H. L., & McDaniel, M. A. (2014). *Make it stick: The science of successful learning.* Cambridge, MA: Harvard University Press.

Burger, E., & Starbird, M. (2012). Igniting insights through mistakes. In *The five elements of effective thinking* (pp. 47–72). Princeton, NJ: Princeton University Press.

Butler, A. (2014). Is immediate feedback always best? [Craig Roberts interview]. *EdSurge.* Retrieved from https://www.edsurge.com/news/2016-02-16-is-immediate-feedback-always-best

Bye, J. (2011, May 5). Desirable difficulties in the classroom [Web log post]. *Psychology Today.* Retrieved from http://www.psychologytoday.com/blog/all-about-addiction/201105/desirable-difficulties-in-the-classroom

Carrithers, D., Ling, T., & Bean, J. C. (2008). Messy problems and lay audiences: Teaching critical thinking within the finance curriculum. *Business Communication Quarterly, 71,* 152–170.

Clariana, R. B., Wagner, D., & Roher Murphy, L. C. (2000). *Educational Technology Research and Development,* 48, 5. https://doi.org/10.1007/BF02319855

Douglass, F. (August 3, 1857). *Emancipation speech, Canandaigua, New York.* Retrieved from https://rbscp.lib.rochester.edu/4398

Doyle, T. (2011). *Learner-centered teaching: Putting the research on learning into practice.* Sterling, VA: Stylus.

Dweck, C., & Leggett, E. (1988). A social-cognitive approach to motivation and personality. *Psychological Review, 95*(2), 256–273.

Edmondson, A. (2011). Strategies for learning from failure. *Harvard Business Review.* Retrieved from https://hbr.org/2011/04/strategies-for-learning-from-failure

Fani, T., & Ghaemi, F. (2011). Implications of Vygotsky's zone of proximal development (ZPD) in teacher education: ZPTD and self-scaffolding. *Procedia—Social and Behavioral Sciences, 29,* 1549–1554. doi:10.1016/j.sbspro.2011.11.396

Foerde, K., & Shohamy, D. (2011). Feedback timing modulates brain systems for learning in humans. *Journal of Neuroscience, 31*(37), 13157–13167. doi:10.1523/JNEUROSCI.2701-11.2011

Hattie, J. (2012). *Visible learning: A synthesis of over 800 meta-analyses.* New York, NY: Routledge.

Hattie, J., & Timperley, H. (2007). The power of feedback. *Review of Educational Research,* 71, 81–112. doi:10.3102/003465430298487

Hmelo-Silver, C., Duncan, R., & Chinn, C. (2007). Scaffolding and achievement in problem-based and inquiry learning: A response to Kirschner, Sweller, and Clark. *Educational Psychologist, 42*(2), 99–107. Retrieved from http://www.tandfonline.com/doi/full/10.1080/00461520701263368?src=recsys

Huddler, M. (2013, October 14). The messy and unpredictable classroom. *Faculty Focus.* Retrieved from https://www.facultyfocus.com/articles/teaching-and-learning/the-messy-and-unpredictable-classroom/

Kapur, M. (2012). Productive failure in learning the concept of variance. *Instructional Science, 40*(4), 651–672. Retrieved from https://link.springer.com/article/10.1007/s11251-012-9209-6

Kapur, M. (2014). Comparing learning from productive failure and vicarious failure. *Journal of Teacher Education, 23*(4), 651–677.

Kapur, M., & Bielaczyc, K. (2012). Designing for productive failure. *Journal of the Learning Sciences, 21,* 45–83.

Kirschner, P., Sweller, J., & Clark, R. E. (2010). Why minimal guidance during instruction does not work: An analysis of the failure of constructivist, discovery, problem-based, experiential, and inquiry-based teaching. *Educational Psychologist,* *41*(2), 75–86. Retrieved from http://www.tandfonline.com/doi/abs/10.1207/ s15326985ep4102_1?src=recsys

Kuh, G. D. (2008). *High-impact educational practices: What they are, who has access to them, and why they matter.* Washington, DC: Association of American Colleges & Universities.

McDaniel, M. A., & Butler, A. C. (1994). A contextual framework for understanding when difficulties are desirable. In A. S. Benjamin (Ed.), *Successful remembering and successful forgetting: A Festschrift in honor of Robert A. Bjork* (pp. 175–199). London, UK: Psychology Press.

Mullet, H., Butler, A., Verdin, B., von Borries, R., & Marsh, E. (2014). Delaying feedback promotes transfer or knowledge despite student preferences to receive feedback immediately. *Journal of Applied Research in Memory and Cognition, 3,* 222–229. doi:10.1016/j.jarmac.2014.05.001

Plank, K. M. (Ed.). (2011). *Team teaching: Across the disciplines, across the academy.* Sterling, VA: Stylus.

Porter, D. (2013). The messy and unpredictable classroom. In M. Huddler, (Ed.), *Faculty focus.* Retrieved from https://www.facultyfocus.com/articles/teaching-and-learning/the-messy-and-unpredictable-classroom/

Roberts, C. (2014). Is immediate feedback always best? *EdSurge.* Retrieved from https://www.edsurge.com/news/2016-02-16-is-immediate-feedback-always-best

Soderstrom, N. (2015, August 4). Take the path of more resistance. *Mastery, Study Tips.* Retrieved from http://www.lastinglearning.com/2015/08/04/desirable-difficulties-path-of-more-resistance/

Soderstrom, N., & Bjork, R. (2013). Learning versus performance. In D. S. Dunn (Ed.), *Oxford Bibliographies Online: Psychology.* New York, NY: Oxford University Press. Retrieved from https://bjorklab.psych.ucla.edu/wp-content/uploads/ sites/13/2016/07/Soderstrom_Bjork_Learning_versus_Performance.pdf

Svinicki, M. (2004). *Learning and motivation in the postsecondary classroom.* Bolton, MA: Anker.

Team-based learning. (n.d.). *Team-based learning collaborative.* Retrieved from http://www.teambasedlearning.org

Weimer, M. (2011). Mastery and performance orientations. In M. Huddler (Ed.), *Faculty Focus.* Retrieved from https://www.facultyfocus.com/articles/teaching-and-learning/mastery-and-performance-orientations/

Wisegeek.org. (n.d.). *What is the connection between long-term memory and critical thinking?* Retrieved from http://www.wisegeek.org/what-is-the-connection-between-long-term-memory-and-critical-thinking.htm

Wolters, C., Yu, S., & Pintrich, P. (1996). The relation between goal orientation and students' motivational beliefs and self-regulated learning. *Learning and Individual Differences, 8*(3), 211–238.

Zull, J. E. (2002). *The art of changing the brain: Enriching the practice of teaching by exploring the biology of learning.* Sterling, VA: Stylus.

Chapter 4.1 Workshop

Bessant, S., Bailey, P., Robinson, Z., Tomkinson, C., Tomkinson, R., Ormerod, R., & Boast, R. (2013). *Problem-based learning: Case study of sustainability education: A toolkit for university educators.* Retrieved from http://www.heacademy.ac.uk/assets/documents/ntfs/Problem_Based_Learning_Toolkit.pdf

Dewey, J. (1956). *The school and society and the child and the curriculum.* Chicago, Illinois: The University of Chicago Press.

Erasmus University. (2012, December 13). Erasmus University College— Problem based learning [YouTube video]. Retrieved from http://www.youtube.com/watch?v=ITjZqK_zhcI

Hmelo-Silver, C. E. (2004). Problem-based learning: What and how do students learn? *Educational Phycology Review, 16*(3), 235–266. doi:10.1023/B:EDPR0000034022.16470.f3

Hoffman, C. (2011, February 16). *Project-based learning explained by Westminster College* [YouTube video]. Retrieved from http://www.youtube.com/watch?v=2KzWu8mQSZo

Luo, Y. (2017, October 13). The influence of problem-based learning on learning effectiveness in students of varying learning abilities within physical education. *Innovations in Education and Teaching International,* 1–11. Retrieved from http://www.tandfonline.com/doi/full/10.1080/14703297.2017.1389288

Lynch, M. (2017, October 13). 7 must-have problem based learning apps, tools, and resources. *The Tech Advocate.* Retrieved from http://www.thetechedvocate.org/7-must-problem-based-learning-apps-tools-resources/

Major, C. H., & Palmer, B. (2001). Assessing the effectiveness of problem-based learning in higher education: Lessons from the literature. *Academic Exchange Quarterly, 5*(1), 4–9.

Schmidt, H., Rotgans, J., & Yew, E. (2011). The process of problem-based learning: What works and why. *Medical Education, 45*(8), 792–806. doi:10.1111/j.1365-2923.2011.04035.x

Strobel, J., & van Barneveld, A. (2009). When is PBL more effective? A meta-synthesis of meta-analyses comparing PBL to conventional classrooms. *Interdisciplinary Journal of Problem-Based Learning, 3*(1), 44–58.

Study Guides and Strategies. (n.d.). *Problem-based learning.* Retrieved from http://www.studygs.net/pbl.htm

Chapter 5

ACT. (2016). *First-generation college students remain far behind peers in college readiness.* Retrieved from http://www.act.org/content/act/en/newsroom/first-generation-college-students-remain-far-behind-peers-in-college-readiness.html

Amelink, C. T. (2005). *Predicting academic success among first-year, first-generation students.* (Published doctoral dissertation from the Virginia Polytechnic Institute

and State University). Retrieved from https://pdfs.semanticscholar.org/fa6f/27b8
fef2debd2424968feedceff4ccc2bdfe.pdf

Chasteen, S. (2017). How can I create community in an active classroom, so that
students feel encouraged to engage? *PhysPort.* Retrieved from https://www
.physport.org/recommendations/Entry.cfm?ID=101221

Elias, M. (2009). The four keys to helping at-risk kids. *Edutopia.* Retrieved from
https://www.edutopia.org/strategies-help-at-risk-students

Fink, L. (2013). *Creating significant learning experiences: An integrated approach to
designing college courses* (2nd ed.). San Francisco, CA: Jossey-Bass.

Gabriel, K. (2008). *Teaching unprepared students: Success and retention strategies.* Sterling, VA: Stylus.

Gross, D., Pietri, E., Anderson, G., Moyanho-Camihort, K., & Graham, M. (2015).
Increased preclass preparation underlies student outcome improvement in the
flipped classroom. *CBE Lifesciences Education, 14*(4), 1–8.

Hardman, D. (2006). Throw away the spoon! Making life difficult for students. *Investigations in University Teaching and Learning, 4*(1), 62–73.

Hogan K., & Eddy, S. (2014). Getting under the hood: How and for whom
does increasing course structure work? *CBE Life Science Education, 13*(3),
453–68.

Hughes, R., & Pace, C. R. (2003). Using NSSE to study student retention and withdrawal. *Assessment Update, 15*(4), 1–2.

Kinzie, J., Gonyea, R., Shoup, R., & Kuh, G. D. (2008). Promoting persistence
and success of underrepresented students: Lessons for teaching and learning. *New
Directions for Teaching and Learning, 115,* 21–38. doi:10.1002/tl.323

Kuh, G. D. (2008). *High-impact educational practices: What they are, who has access
to them, and why they matter.* Washington DC: Association of American Colleges
& Universities.

Kuh, G. D., Kinzie, J., Buckley, J. A., Bridge, B. K., & Hayek, J. C. (2006). What
matters to student success: A review of the literature. *Commissioned Report for the
"National Symposium on Postsecondary Student Success: Spearheading a Dialog on
Student Success," 151.* Retrieved from https://nces.ed.gov/npec/pdf/Kuh_Team_
ExecSumm.pdf

Lam, P., Srivatsan, T., Doverspike, D., Vesalo, J., & Mawasha, P. (2005). A ten-year
assessment of the pre-engineering program for under-represented, low income
and/or first generation college students at The University of Akron. *The Journal
of STEM Education: Innovations and Research, 6.3*(4), 14–20.

Lewis, G., Holland, P., & Kelly, K. (1992). Working-class students speak out. *The
Radical Teacher, 42,* 10–12.

Longanecker, D. (2013). *New report projects high school graduating classes will be
smaller, more diverse.* Western Interstate for Higher Education. Retrieved from
https://www.prnewswire.com/news-releases/new-report-projects-high-school-
graduating-classes-will-be-smaller-more-diverse-186335072.html

Lyons, A. C. (2004). A profile of financially at-risk college students. *Journal of Consumer Affairs, 38*(1), 56–81.

NCES. (2017). Undergraduate retention and graduate rates. *The Condition of Education 2017* (NCES 2017-144). Retrieved from https://nces.ed.gov/programs/coe/indicator_ctr.asp

Parsad, B., & Lewis, L. (2003). *Remedial education at degree-granting postsecondary institutions in fall 2000 (NCES 2004-010)*. National Center for Education Statistics, Institute of Education Sciences. Washington DC: U.S. Department of Education.

Paul, A. M. (2014, March 21). What's the 'sweet spot' of difficulty for learning. *Mind/Shift: How We Will Learn*. Retrieved from https://ww2.kqed.org/mindshift/2014/03/21/whats-the-sweet-spot-of-difficulty-for-learning/

Pell Institute. (2008). *Moving beyond access: College success for low income, first-generation students*. Retrieved from http://www.pellinstitute.org/publications-Moving_Beyond_Access_2008.shtml

Pennebaker, J., Gosling, S., & Ferrell, J. (2014). Daily online testing in large classes: Boosting college performance while reducing achievement gaps. *PLOS ONE*, *8*(11), e79774. Retrieved from 110.1371/journal.pone.00797748.doi:10.1371/journal.pone.0079774

Rendon, L. I. (1994). Validating culturally diverse students: Toward a new model of learning and student development. *Innovative Higher Education*, *19*(1), 33–51.

Schilling, K. M., & Schilling, K. L. (2005). Expectations and performance. In M. L. Upcraft, J. N. Gardner, & B. O. Barefoot (Eds.), *Challenging and supporting the first-year student: A handbook for improving the first year of college* (pp. 108–124). San Francisco, CA: Jossey-Bass.

Stahl, N., Simpson, M., & Hayes, C. (1992). Ten recommendations from research for teaching high-risk college students. *Journal of Developmental Education*, *16*(1), 10–12. Retrieved from https://ncde.appstate.edu/sites/ncde.appstate.edu/files/Reprinted%20from%20the%20Journal%20of%20Developmental%20Education.pdf

Tate, E. (2017, April 26). Graduation rates and race. *Inside Higher Ed*. Retrieved from https://www.insidehighered.com/news/2017/04/26/college-completion-rates-vary-race-and-ethnicity-report-finds

Wang, H., & Grimes, J. W. (2001). A systematic approach to assessing retention programs: Identifying critical points for meaningful interventions and validating outcomes assessment. *Journal College Student Retention*, *2*(1), 59–68.

Chapter 5.1 Workshop

Bandy, J. (2018). *What is service learning or community engagement?* Vanderbilt Center for Teaching. Retrieved from https://cft.vanderbilt.edu/guides-sub-pages/teaching-through-com

Boyer, E. (1996). The scholarship of engagement. *Bulletin of the American Academy of Arts and Sciences*, *1*(1), 18–33.

Bringle, R., Philips, M., & Hudson, M. (2004). *The measure of service learning: Research scales to assess student experiences.* Washington DC: American Psychological Association.

Campus Compact. (2003). *Introduction to service learning toolkit: Readings and resources for faculty.* Retrieved from http://compact.org/resource-type/syllabi/

Centre College. (n.d.). *Community-based learning.* Retrieved from http://ctl.centre .edu/community-based-learning.html

Correia, M., & Bleicher, R. (2008). Making connections to teach reflection. *Michigan Journal of Community Service Learning, 14*(12), 41–49.

Felten, P., Gilchrist, L. Z., & Darby, A. (2006). Emotion and learning: Feeling our way toward a new theory of reflection in service-learning. *Michigan Journal of Community Service Learning, 12*(2), 38–46.

Hammersley, L. (2013). Community-based service-learning: Partnerships of reciprocal exchange? Asia-Pacific. *Journal of Cooperative Education, 14*(3), 171–184.

Hatcher, J. A., Bringle, R. G., & Muthiah, R. (2004). Designing effective reflection: What matters to service-learning? *Michigan Journal of Community Service Learning, 11*(1), 38–46. Retrieved from http://hdl.handle.net/2027/ spo.3239521.0011.104

Hogan, K., & Eddy, S. (2014). Getting under the hood: How and for whom does increasing course structure work? *CBE Life Science Education, 13*(3), 453–68.

Jacoby, B. (Ed.). (1996). *Service-learning in higher education.* San Francisco, CA: Jossey-Bass.

Meader, L. (2011). Real money, real lessons, *Colby Magazine, 100*(2). doi: 1410.1371/ journal.pone.007977417

Pennebaker, J., Gosling, S., & Ferrell, J. (2014). Daily online testing in large classes: Boosting college performance while reducing achievement gaps. *PLOS ONE, 8*(11), e79774. Retrieved from 110.1371/journal.pone.00797748doi:10.1371/ journal.pone.0079774

Prusinski, E., & Wells, S. (2015–2016). *Community based learning at Centre College: Faculty handbook.* Retrieved from http://ctl.centre.edu/assets/cblhandbook.pdf

Chapter 6

Brownell, S. E., & Tanner, K. D. (2012). Barriers to faculty pedagogical change: Lack of training, time, incentives, and . . . tensions with professional identity? *CBE Life Science Education, 11*, 339–346. Retrieved from http://www.lifescied .org/content/11/4/339.full?ijkey=9e1354a504e56f0223f33fb0a677c708a53f4e4 8&keytype2=tf_ipsecsha

Chapman, E. (2003). Alternative approaches to assessing student engagement rates. *Practical Assessment, Research & Evaluation, 8*(13), 1–7.

Chasteen, S. (2017). How can I create community in an active classroom, so that students feel encouraged to engage? *PhysPort.* Retrieved from https://www.physport .org/recommendations/Entry.cfm?ID=101221

Clark, D., & Redmond, M. (1982). *Small group instructional diagnosis: Final report.* Retrieved from https://eric.ed.gov/?id=ED217954

Cohen, P. A. (1980). Effectiveness of student-rating feedback for improving college instruction: A meta-analysis of findings. *Research in Higher Education, 13,* 321–341.

Cook-Sather, A. (2009). An alternative framework for conceptualizing and supporting school reform efforts. *Educational Theory, 59*(2), 217–231. doi:10.111 1/j.1741-5446.2009.00315.

Croxall, B. (2012, April 3). Improve your course evaluations by having your class write letters to future students. *Chronicle of Higher Education.* Retrieved from http://www.chronicle.com/blogs/profhacker/improve-your-course-evaluations-by-having-your-class-write-letters-to-future-students/48659

Ellis, P. (2013). *Evidence-based practice in nursing.* New York, NY: Sage.

Felder, R. M. (2007). Sermons for grumpy campers. *Chemical Engineering Education, 41,* 183–184.

Felder, R. M. (2011). Hang in there! Dealing with student resistance to learner-centered teaching. *Chemical Engineering Education, 43,* 131–132.

Felder, R. M., & Brent, R. (1996). Navigating the bumpy road to student-centered instruction. *College Teaching, 44*(2), 43–47. Retrieved from http://www4.ncsu.edu/unity/lockers/users/f/felder/public/Papers/Resist.html

Felder, R. M., & Brent, R. (2016). Common active learning mistakes. In *Teaching and learning STEM: A practical guide* (pp. 122–125). San Francisco, CA: Jossey-Bass. doi:10.1177/2372732215624708

Kaufman, D., Felder, R., & Fuller, H. (1999). Peer ratings in cooperative learning teams. *Proceedings of the 1999 Annual ASEE Meeting.* Retrieved from http://www4.ncsu.edu/unity/lockers/users/f/felder/public/Papers/kaufman-asee.PDF

Kornell, N. (2009). Optimising learning using flashcards: Spacing is more effective than cramming. *Applied Cognitive Psychology, 23,* 1297–1317. doi:10.1002/acp.1537

Lewis, R. (2001). Classroom discipline and student responsibility: The students' view. *Teaching and Teacher Education, 17,* 307–319. Retrieved from http://passionatelearning.pbworks.com/f/lewis.pdf

Nguyen, K. A., Borrego, M. J., Finelli, C., Shekhar, P., DeMonbrun, R. M., Henderson, C., Prince, M. J., & Waters, C. (2016, June 26–June 29). Measuring student response to instructional practices (StRIP) in traditional and active classrooms. In *2016 ASEE Annual Conference and Exposition.* New Orleans, LA: American Society for Engineering Education.

Nilson, L. B. (2016). *Teaching at its best: A research-based resource for college instructors* (4th ed.). San Francisco, CA: Jossey-Bass.

Pfaff, E., & Huddleston, P. (2003). Does it matter if I hate teamwork? *Journal of Marketing Education, 25*(1), 37–45.

Pintrich, P. (2003). A motivational science perspective on the role of student motivation in learning and teaching contexts. *Journal of Educational Psychology, 95*(4), 667–686. Retrieved from http://blog.sciencegeekgirl.com/wp-content/uploads/2012/05/pintrich-motivation-review.pdf

Richmond, V. P., & McCroskey, J. C. (1992). *Communication: Apprehension, avoidance, and effectiveness* (3rd ed.). Scottsdale, AZ: Gorsuch Scarisbrick.

Sayre, E. (n.d.). "Stop-Go-Change" form. Retrieved from https://www.physport .org/recommendations/files/Stop-Go-Change-Evals.pdf

Seidel, S., & Tanner, K. (2013). Approaches to biology teaching and learning "What if students revolt?"—Considering student resistance: Origins, options, and opportunities for investigation. *CBE—Life Sciences Education, 12*, 586–595.

Shekhar, P., Demonbrun, M., Borrego, M., Finelli, C., Prince, M., Henderson, C., & Waters, C. (2015). Development of an observation protocol to study undergraduate engineering student resistance to active learning. *International Journal of Engineering Education, 31*(2), 597–609.

Shernoff, D. (2013). *Optimal learning environments to promote student engagement.* New York, NY: Springer. Retrieved from https://link.springer.com/ book/10.1007/978-1-4614-7089-2

Sorenson, D. L. (2001). College teachers and student consultants: Collaborating about teaching and learning. In D. Miller (Ed.), *Student-assisted teaching: A guide to faculty-student teamwork* (pp. 179–183). Bolton, MA: Ankar.

Teach it Slant (n.d.). *Tuesday tips: The plus-delta chart.* Retrieved from https:// teachitslant.com/2013/06/04/tuesday-tips-the-plus-delta-chart/

Tolman, A. O., & Kremling, J. (Eds.). (2016). *Why students resist learning: A practical model for understanding and helping students.* Sterling, VA: Stylus.

University of California, San Francisco. (n.d.). *Plus-delta Template.* Retrieved from http://fhop.ucsf.edu/sites/fhop.ucsf.edu/files/custom_download/ACPS_Plus_ Delta_Template.pdf

University of Colorado, Boulder. (2013). Framing the interactive engagement classroom. *Boulder: Science Education Initiative.* Retrieved from www.colorado.edu/ sei/fac-resources/framing.html

Zhao, N., Wardeska, J., McGuire, S., & Cook, E. (2014). Metacognition: An effective tool to promote success in college science learning. *Journal of College Science Teaching, 43*(4), 48–54. Retrieved from http://www.deltastate.edu/PDFFiles/ Academic%20Affairs/teaching-and-learning-resources/metacognition-an-effective-tool.pdfm

Appendix

Aune, B. (2002). Teaching action research via distance. *Journal of Technology and Teacher Education, 10*(2008), 461–479.

Babson Survey Research Group. (2015). *Online report card: Tracking online education in the United States.* Retrieved from https://onlinelearningconsortium.org/read/ online-report-card-tracking-online-education-united-states-2015/

Bell, M. & Farrier, S. (2008) Measuring success in e-learning: A multi-dimensional approach. *The Electronic Journal of eLearning, 6*(2), 99–110. Retrieved from www.ejel.org/issue/download.html?idArticle=62

Buck, J. (2001). Assuring quality in distance education. *Higher Education in Europe, 26*, 599–602.

Coyner, S. C., & McCann, P. L. (2004). Advantages and challenges of teaching in an electronic environment: The accommodate model. *International Journal of Instructional Media, 31*, 223–228.

Davison, M. M. (2005). Distance education in high schools: Benefits, challenges, and suggestions. *The Clearing House, 78*, 105–108.

Deal, W. F. III. (2002). Distance learning: Teaching technology online. *The Technology Teacher, 61*, 21–26.

Domun, M. & Goonesh, B. (2014). *Effectiveness of a self assessment tool on an e-learning platform.* Saarbrucken, Germany: LAP Lambert Academic Publishing

Everson, M. (2009, September). 10 things I've learned about teaching online. *ELearn Magazine.* Retrieved from http://elearnmag.acm.org/featured.cfm?aid= 1609990

Frazier, A., & Hooper, C. R. (2012). *From lab to classroom: Implementing desirable difficulties to increase acquisition of foundational knowledge.* Retrieved from https://ashleyonteaching.files.wordpress.com/2012/02/lilly-2012-amf-crh.ppsx

Friedman, J. (2016, February 9). Enrollment in online learning up, except at for-profits. *U. S. News and World Report.* Retrieved from: https://www.usnews.com/ education/online-education/articles/2016-02-09/study-enrollment-in-online-learning-up-except-at-for-profits

Gillett-Swan, J. (2017). The challenges of online learning supporting and engaging the isolated learner. *Journal of Learning Design, 10*(1), 20–30. Retrieved from https://www.jld.edu.au/article/download/293/293-749-1-PB.pdf

Karber, D. J. (2003). Comparisons and contrasts in traditional versus on-line teaching in management. *Higher Education in Europe, 26*, 533–536.

Kumar, S. (2015, July 10). 5 common problems faced by students in eLearning and how to overcome them. *ELearning Industry.* Retrieved from https:// elearningindustry.com/5-common-problems-faced-by-students-in-elearning-overcome

Li, C., & Irby, B. (2008). An overview of online education: Attractiveness, benefits, challenges, concerns, and recommendations. *College Student Journal Part A, 42*(2), 449–458.

Lyons, J. F. (2004). Teaching U.S. history online: Problems and prospects. *The History Teacher, 37*, 447–456.

Mesa Community College. (2017). *Teaching an online course: The big picture.* Retrieved from http://ctl.mesacc.edu/teaching/designing-an-online-course/

Nilson, L., & Goodson, L. (2017). *Online teaching at its best: Merging instructional design with teaching and learning research.* San Francisco, CA: Jossey-Bass.

Open Culture. (2017). *MOOCs from great universities.* Retrieved from http://www .openculture.com/free_certificate_courses

Singh, P., & Pan, W. (2004). Online education: Lessons for administrators and instructors. *College Student Journal, 38*, 302–308.

Song, L., Singleton, E., Hill, J., & Koh, M. (2004). Improving online learning: Student perceptions of useful and challenging characteristics. *The Internet and Higher Education, 7,* 59–70. doi:10.1016/j.iheduc.2003.11.003

ABOUT THE AUTHORS

Diane Cummings Persellin is the Murchison Professor of Music Education at Trinity University in San Antonio, Texas. In 2017 she received the Z.T. Scott Faculty Fellowship, Trinity University's highest award for teaching. Her research and teaching interests include teacher education and professional development.

Mary Blythe Daniels is the Stodghill Professor of Spanish at Centre College in Danville, Kentucky. In 2015 she was awarded the Kentucky CASE Professor of the year. Her research and teaching interests include early modern Spanish theater and gender studies.

Persellin and Daniels coauthored *A Concise Guide to Improving Student Learning: Six Evidence-Based Principles and How to Apply Them* (Stylus Publishing, 2014).

but also in research and creative work. *A Concise Guide to Improving Student Learning* reviews, condenses, and explains those theories and practices—allowing you, the reader, to efficiently and effectively engage with those ideas."
—**Michael Reder**, *Director, Joy Shechtman Mankoff Faculty Center for Teaching & Learning, Connecticut College*

Acknowledging the growing body of peer-reviewed literature on practices that can dramatically impact teaching, this intentionally brief book:

- Summarizes recent research on six of the most compelling principles in learning and teaching
- Describes their application to the college classroom
- Presents teaching strategies that are based on pragmatic practices
- Provides annotated bibliographies and important citations for faculty who want to explore these topics further

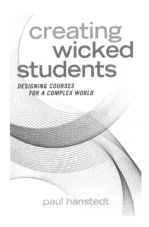

Creating Wicked Students

Designing Courses for a Complex World

Paul Hanstedt

This is a course design book centered on the idea that the goal in the college classroom—in all classrooms, all the time—is to develop students who are not just loaded with content, but capable of using that content in thoughtful, deliberate ways to make the world a better place. Achieving this goal requires a top-to-bottom reconsideration of courses, including student learning goals, text selection and course structure, day-to-day pedagogies, and assignment and project design. *Creating Wicked Students* takes readers through each step of the process, providing multiple examples at each stage, while always encouraging instructors to consider concepts and exercises in light of their own courses and students.

22883 Quicksilver Drive
Sterling, VA 20166-2019   Subscribe to our e-mail alerts: www.Styluspub.com

Also available from Stylus

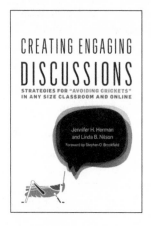

Creating Engaging Discussions

Strategies for "Avoiding Crickets" in Any Size Classroom and Online

Jennifer H. Herman and Linda B. Nilson

Foreword by Stephen D. Brookfield

"*Creating Engaging Discussions* examines one of the most challenging parts of teaching—designing and managing discussion activities that engage students while contributing meaningfully to their learning. Faculty members will love the way the book addresses their common instructional challenges with a mix of evidence-based principles, use-it-on-Monday activities, and in-depth case studies. Educational developers will appreciate its scholarly background and suggestions for using the book within reading groups and workshops. A must-have addition for your bookshelf." — *Greg Siering, PhD, Director, Center for Innovative Teaching and Learning, Indiana University Bloomington*

If you have ever been apprehensive about initiating classroom discussion, fearing silences, the domination of a couple of speakers, superficial contributions, or off-topic remarks, this book provides strategies for creating a positive learning experience.

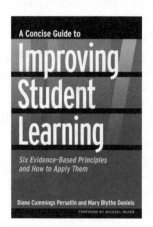

A Concise Guide to Improving Student Learning

Six Evidence-Based Principles and How to Apply Them

Diane Cummings Persellin and Mary Blythe Daniels

Foreword by Michael Reder

"The options and resources for improving one's teaching sometime feel limitless and overwhelming, especially for faculty members who are busily engaged not only in teaching and service,

(Continues on preceding page)